A Mirror for The Blind

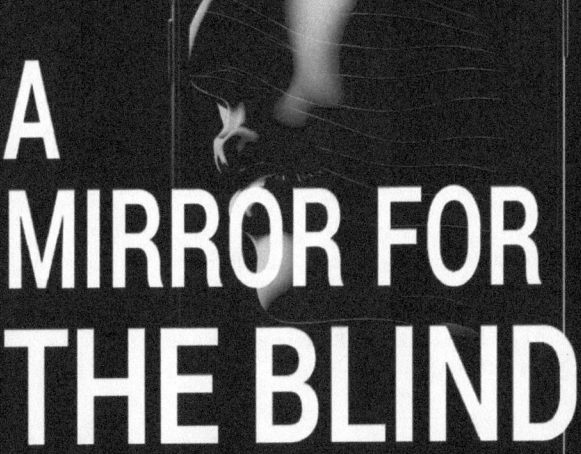

A MIRROR FOR THE BLIND

Reflections of a Digital Seoul

A Novel by

JEONG MU

METRIC PUBLISHER

Copyright © 2023 by Jeong-mu
All rights reserved.
ISBN: 979-11-982002-3-5

All rights reserved.
No part of this publication may be reproduced, distributed, or transmitted in any form or by any means, including photocopying, recording, or other electronic or mechanical methods, without the prior written permission of the publisher, except as permitted by U.S. copyright law. For permission requests, contact [zero.proof.all@gmail.com].

Translated by Mark Allen Brazeal
Inspected by Charles Luskin
Book Design by Hayoung Wee
Illustrations by A.H.

First Printing, 2023

METRIC Publisher
3516, 3rd floor, 15-1, Achasan-ro 7-gil
Seongdong-gu, Seoul, 04793

For my family,

K.J. Park, S.D. Jeong, J.S. Jeong, Concepcion Sluder,

and for anyone who holds their own Earth on shoulders.

Preface

I remember as a freshman in college using my newly-issued student ID to try registering for a social network reserved exclusively for students at my university. It made me feel special, important even, to be granted access to this online space that no one else could enter unless they were a member of our school, "our" being an important demarcation in Korea for membership in key in-groups at the expense of excluding others, like speakers of our language or members of our people and our nation. What can I say, it felt good to be "in." But it didn't take long for this initial positivity and pride to curdle into bitterness. The message boards were populated with cynical jokes from older students, confronted by students who were younger and smarter or went to better schools, and derisive comments about how no one would have chosen this school if they hadn't screwed up on an important test or two along the way. The daily posts of our classmates became a relentless torrent of complaints that quickly faded to a dull white noise.

As I watched the turbulent wave of my 20s crash and be absorbed into the wider sea of life, I prepared for early adulthood's final rite of passage: to secure stable employment at a company. It was at that moment that I found myself joining yet another social network, this time an anonymous online community for office workers. This time, to register you needed a business card and an official company email. I imagined the sense of pride I would feel having an address from a "big corporation" next to my profile. This was just one of the little fantasies a naive new employee like me entertained before learning any better.

But even that small bit of pride came crashing down sooner than expected. I immediately encountered the bitter taste of being judged not only for my educational background and job, but also for my assets, looks, and even who I might marry. As part of the registration process, to be "verified" you either needed to work for a well-known company or be an accredited specialist. Telling people you worked for a lesser company was like patently presenting your Achilles heel. Then, in February 2022, following the aftermath of COVID-19, which sent shockwaves through asset markets, the social network became an even bigger battleground for such short-sighted judgment and criticism.

By the time I got used to the taste of my bitterness, I also came to the realization that adulthood was merely a change from one state to another in a great cycle of repetition; from school to company; report card to performance report; lover to spouse. Verification became a source of envy with everyone trying to take the successes of those around them and spin them as their own. It was basically high school all over again, with students using Photoshop to falsify their college entrance exam scores to receive whatever little bit of verification from the community they could.

Like cheap gold leaf, we present ourselves online not according to who we really are, but based on our perceptions of how we think the top 5% of earners live. We constantly compare ourselves to these hallucinations, perpetuating a culture of always trying to "live like them," while never truly portraying ourselves for who we really are. Those unable to fit this image feel constantly deprived, while those who seem to belong live under the constant fear of being ousted one day. The "theys" line everyone up, judge them for all they are worth and start picking the losers.

With this novel, I wanted to reveal the social structure that supports this sort of "live like them" culture. It fosters a form of mediocrity far more mundane than would have been produced on its own, and I want to alert people to the real sense of deprivation it inspires. I hope we reach a point where we are able to simply and casually encourage one another in whatever lives we choose to live and support the worlds that we each create.

However, I also understand we live in a world where sometimes the only sustenance to be had is by munching on stale cereal without any milk to wash it down. And yet, every day after work, riding the bus home, or just before falling asleep, I can't help but hear a whisper telling me that the quieter, sweeter life is the one we are already living in.

I hope even a plain and insipid life will be sought after like the occasional soggy cereal marshmallow. Our unquenchable thirst for exchanging mutual "likes" online has got to subside someday. Like the sound of the wind blowing through a park or a tail light reflected in the window of a bus, or a cup of coffee that cleanses the palate, I long for the kind of life where you can simply focus on your own two feet on the ground in front of you.

To the government workers that spend their time untying our twisted knots, or the scholars walking upon their sea of truths, to anyone that wakes up and faces the mirror in front of them, I hope this writing becomes one tiny pebble in what will eventually form a mountain.

Sweeping up the ashes,
October 2022

Contents

Preface　　　　　　　　　　　　　　　　7

Just a Moment!　　　　　　　　　　　13
Should I Just Learn to Code?　　　　　29
The Bridle　　　　　　　　　　　　　49
The Mistake　　　　　　　　　　　　68
The Last Train　　　　　　　　　　　85
Freedom　　　　　　　　　　　　　99
The One Left Behind　　　　　　　　115
The Rubik's Cube　　　　　　　　　146
Hanging from the Cliff　　　　　　　173
A Mirror for The Blind　　　　　　　203

About the Author

The story, all names, characters, and incidents portrayed in this production are fictitious. No identification with actual persons (living or deceased), places, buildings, and products are intended or should be inferred and any resemblance to real persons, living or dead, is purely coincidental.

Just a Moment!

"Just a moment!"

At least two more can fit if everyone just squeezes in a bit. I push my way into the already-packed elevator—Assistant Manager Youngbaek Kim, thirty-two years old, and in my fifth year at P Corporation, the company with the second highest market capitalization in Korea. Occupying the last available space in the elevator before the doors close, I stand there stiffly, like a gatekeeper. Right as the doors are about to close and allow the elevator to deliver everyone to their homes after a long day of work, a single voice is heard crying out from down the hall.

"Just... just a moment!"

The sound of urgent, heavy footsteps squeaking down the hallway. An anxious, expectant face twisted with dilemma flashes in between the narrow opening. Expressions sharp with disappointment and a few grumbles spread throughout the elevator. Fortunately, this tardy would-be rider suddenly hesitates and the doors silently close in his face before he can board.

Heavy with the defeat of the day, I feel my only sense of victory right here in the elevator. I let out a sigh and promise myself to leave five minutes earlier tomorrow.

Inside the elevator, everything is quiet as the occupants begin to shed their corporate personas for the day. This muted ceremony is interrupted when the robotic voice of the elevator breaks the silence to announce our arrival at our destination in the crisp, clear speech of an automated message.

"Welcome to the first floor. You may now exit."

Heard daily, this simple welcome sentence is the sound of liberation to the exhausted riders.

Everyone exchanges farewells as we exit one by one through the revolving doors at the front of the building. From the moment I was employed as a new recruit, to what I hope will be my slow but eventual rise to the position of executive, these revolving doors will greet me every single day of my commute. Today, the doors feel as heavy as the weight of my thirty-two years.

Everyone stuffs their employee IDs deep down into their bags as they walk away from the building. Just as mankind slowly began to erect its spine long ago in our evolutionary past, my colleagues and I proudly stretch our shoulders and straighten our backs the farther we move from our workplace. Was it the weight of the name tags around our necks that caused our bodies to bow so low?

For a moment the straightening of my spine slingshots me forward, almost like a spring. Everyone walks down the sidewalk with their smartphones in hand. The vanguard of employees who left work a moment earlier than everyone else is already waiting in line at the bus stop.

"Mr. Youngbaek, sir!"

It is the voice of twenty-eight-year-old Jungwoo Lee, the youngest member of our team, and the possessor of both a winning personality and a strong desire to please. He still spends most of his time at work bowing incessantly to his senior colleagues while greeting every single person in the office and is the kind of person that avoids making faux pas or awkward social situations to a fault. I don't know how much he suffers inside because of it, but he is extremely well-thought-of around the office. Maybe it's just me, but I'm a little wary of people who don't know how to let loose every once in a while...

"Oh, Jungwoo. Looks like you're going out tonight?"
"Yes, I'm meeting someone nearby. Going straight home, sir?"
"I was thinking about hitting the gym.'"
"On top of it, as always. Oh, this is my bus. Good evening!"

Our youngest member, Jungwoo, always affable and accommodating. I am constantly impressed by how he virtually never loses his composure, no matter the situation. I still forget to address him with the requisite honorific title and end up casually calling him by his first name. We've known each other for how long now and he still calls me "sir." I mean, I know I'm his senior, but a lot of companies are trying to do away with that old-school hierarchy stuff these days, anyway.

Waiting for the bus, I withdraw my unsuspecting phone from my pocket and begin to thumb it for no reason. Seeing I have no messages is like coming home to a lonesome, empty mailbox. Feeling awkward, I quickly take out my earbuds and jam them in my ears.

A message that the bus will be arriving in three minutes flashes across the electronic display of the bus stop. The people waiting crane their necks to gain first sight of their buses long before they are visible. When my bus comes, it halts a little beyond the bus stop itself, as though already in a hurry to leave. Everyone rushes down the sidewalk to catch up to it, myself included. Inside, the bus is brimming with people like so many grains of steamed rice neatly pushed down into the shape of a bowl. Then, just as the doors begin to close, blocking out the sound of a blaring horn, a desperate voice can be heard:

"Just a moment!"

I shoot arrows from my eyes at the bus driver in the mirror. Why should he stop to let another would-be rider onto the bus, still visibly running from so far away? The bus, pretty much near its bursting point, begins to feel all the more cramped on account of this excessively magnanimous gesture on the part of the driver shown to this random latecomer. Why stop to let him on like that? That guy should have waited in line earlier or taken the next bus. I give another angry look at the bus driver, which goes entirely unnoticed.

Now that the bus has crossed over the bridge from the newer, corporate hub that was built south of the river, called Gangnam, to the older, residential and retail districts north of the river, or *Gangbuk*, there is enough room for people to take out their phones again. I instinctively lower the brightness on my screen, even though no one could possibly care enough to take a peek my way.

Time to check "SCR33N."

SCR33N is a social networking app for office workers that requires users to verify their identities using an official corporate email. All the posts are anonymous, with only the name of your workplace visible and usernames given at random. I navigate my way to the hidden folder in my phone I made specifically to hide the fact that I use SCR33N from my coworkers and press the app icon. Using it is discouraged and considered an act of disloyalty by the management and employees. Still, virtually every office worker at least downloads the app once to see what it's all about. Then they either have to feign ignorance or completely hide the fact that they use it on a regular basis, like me. I've opened the app so many times, the thumbnail image might have rubbed off my phone by now. I quickly skim through the feed, narrow slits for eyes, scanning each backlogged post like so many cars stuck in traffic on an endless ribbon of road.

> *"Tell me, do I make the cut?"*
> *"Hey ladies, I'm five foot nine, slim, moderately handsome..."*
> *"Do these qualifications make me marriage material?*
> *My parents keep riding me to get married!"*
> *"Forget all about dating unless you pull in at least $150,000 a year."*
> *"Please, tell me what to do then!"*

How can these people talk about themselves in such cringe-worthy ways when their coworkers might easily take a guess and figure out who they are? No one would ever, ever advertise themself so honestly in a job interview like they do in this app. I guess desperate people are forced to search for love even on an anonymous app like SCR33N. With the simple swipe of my thumb, I instantly feel the familiar sense of false camaraderie that can only be shared by two nameless, anonymous people. Before we started looking down at our screens, we used to have to face our loneliness head-on. Now with the press of a button, we routinely feel this fabricated connection with complete strangers any spare moment of the day. Why does it have to be that technology continues to evolve while humankind fails to get any better? Swiping down to refresh my feed, an endless list of posts falls like so many soda cans from a vending machine, clunking and rattling as they drop down.

Snooping around other sections of the app, I see that posts on the stock market are as ubiquitous as always. One poster with an indistinguishable username that might as well have been a barcode left a message saying he has been volunteering at a company for free for years. The comment section, too, was always a battleground, with posts like: "What kind of imbecile buys high and sells low?" I exhale sharply to stifle a laugh–a little bit too loudly–suddenly aware that I am, in fact, hurtling down the road in a bus completely filled with people.

I'm suddenly reminded of a sentiment often shared on SCR33N, about how regular savings or deposit accounts are the tools of the financially blind. Yet, at least part of the golden fiscal future promised by all these armchair economists, with their encouragement to diversify beyond mere savings accounts by investing in stocks and cryptocurrencies, now seems to face a dark line of ominous clouds gathering on the horizon. I heard somewhere that when interest rates are low, there's little to gain from simply keeping money in the bank. I quickly switch over to my brokerage app using a single, fluid swipe revealing how often I check it per day, even though using the app has been a completely unprofitable investment of my time. I close my eyes, take a deep breath, and look down.

"$50."

The current price of my main stock investment rests at $50. My buds start to slip out from a drip of sweat that gathers in my ear canal.

Around the same time last year, when the price was at $85 a share, every office worker across the country became a financial expert overnight. We took turns sharing random headlines clipped from the news and collaged into indecipherable messages about how well the stock was doing. Everyone's projection was for it to go up to $100. I got caught up in the fervor and ended up firing all of my guns at once on this single stock, even though I know that they say that's not what you're supposed to do. I invested my entire savings from four years of work. Now I recall with endless regret having been convinced by, and even myself repeating such banalities as, "You only live once." and "Don't miss the bus!"

Not long after, the SCR33N community started calling people like me who bought in at that time "residents of the 85th floor," since we were the "lucky ones" who bought in when it was still cheap. Back then, everyone was highly confident that at a price of $85, the stock was a steal. If only I were still stuck on the 85th floor and hadn't taken the express elevator down to the 50th. My left thumb, hovering above my phone, begins to go numb from the pressure of my left shoulder against the handrail. I shift my weight to accommodate the discomfort.

Only a few years ago, I would also recite unfamiliar economic terms like "P/E Ratio" and "EPS" at lunchtime to my coworkers with a serious look on my face. We would talk over each other saying things none of us really knew the first thing about. It didn't matter then. We were the ones in the know, ahead of the rest of the pack, possessing the knowledge necessary to make easy money outside of our boring day jobs.

Now look. All that money I had saved over four years of work might as well have been fuel for a dumpster fire. Only the ashes and an acrid taste of smoke lingered somewhere deep in the back of my throat along with the memory of all the hours I put in gone to waste.

No, now I know the truth; even if this stock that I so dearly wished would float up somewhere above $100 a share were, by some miracle, to eventually make it there, I would still never be able to buy my own house in Seoul. Not in this market. Perhaps if I could somehow reinvent myself as a financial guru and make money selling spurious investment advice, then it might be possible to see a slight uptick in the line graph that is my life.

"The next stop is the Hwayang Intersection."

The same electronic voice from the elevator speaks over the heads of the bus riders. Of course, a person like me who pays the fare and takes the ride can't just get off before everyone else does. It's not that easy to find a seat that will take you all the way. Whether bus rides or stock investments, I can't just get off whenever it's convenient. This does happen to be my stop, however. Like a spoon dipping into a bowl packed with rice, springy at first and then yielding, I push my way politely through the mass of passengers, positioning myself where the doors are. The image suddenly comes to mind that people streaming out of a bus and selling off a hyped-up stock really aren't all that different. Moments before we arrive at my stop, I imagine a scenario where my feet barely touch the pavement and a sudden feeling of vertigo hits me as the bus plows on to its next destination. I see an image of myself in my mind breathing in a cloud of exhaust as the bus pulls away and thinking about how my own portfolio is moving just as far back in the other direction.

"Wait! Just a moment!"

The driver didn't even stop long enough to let anyone off! Shaken from my reverie, I shoot another bevy of arrows at the bus driver in the mirror. He completely blew past my stop, even though I was waiting at the doors to get off. I mean, I pushed the button and everything! My scowl in his mirror goes unnoticed again. Guess I'll have to get off at the next stop. Taking advantage of the extra ten minutes of commute, I post some measly bit of gossip on SCR33N. The buds in my ears start slipping again.

Thanks to the driver, my commute home takes an extra twenty minutes. Getting off at the next stop means I have to walk through the traditional open-air market in my neighborhood to arrive at my front door. At this time of day, the market is bustling with the middle-aged and elderly nabbing last-minute groceries. The stalls line either side of a long pedestrian lane sheltered by a vaulted roof to keep out the rain. It's a relic from the past, but the deals here are cheaper than the multilevel, air-conditioned supermarkets where younger people shop. The fruits sitting in the baskets are thousands of Won cheaper than those in the big stores. A handwritten price tag dangles in front of each basket. Plastic bags droop next to the fruit, hot from sitting outside all day in the sun. The smell of fermented beans, fish, and sesame oil invades my nostrils. I climb the stairs to my one-room studio on the third floor of the building. As soon as the electronic lock slides home, I'm inside and lying down. Today was another exhausting day. My team leader forced me to take over a new set of files, which is extra work that I don't need and shouldn't have to do. Still, when a storm like this hits, I'm usually the type to hunker down in my cellar and wait for it to pass instead of forcing a confrontation. Grateful to be back from another day on the battlefield, grateful to finally return to my normal self, I am simply grateful to be inside my own room and finally lying down.

I turn my head a fraction and the clock reads 7:15. It's time to spy on how other people spend their time after work. Emerging from my single moment of alone time, I flick through the app on my phone to ride the ripples of other lives on social media.

Snapping photos of their fitness journeys–indoor rock climbing, running, finishing up exercise routines–going out for drinks, looking for places to eat... what colorful little fragments of life these images on my screen offer. I'm suddenly reminded of the words of Charlie Chaplin, who said that all life is a tragedy when seen close-up, but a comedy from afar. If Charlie was on social media, what would he post about tonight? Like a raft drifting down a river, I lay flat, letting the flow of my news feed take me where it will.

Even here, alone in my shabby studio apartment, I can't help but obsess over the opinions of others online. I decide to drag my heavy body to the gym, thinking it would probably be better to run on the treadmill rather than have nothing to post myself. Yes, I have to run tonight. I'll even wear my favorite running shoes and joggers. That will make for a decent post to get my daily dose of verification for the day.

I trudge through my workout. When I run on a treadmill like this, closing my eyes, it's the only time I feel like I can experience the full weight of my body. I try imagining that each step brings me closer to my dreams and desires. That I am actually getting better and healthier, and that with each step, I am that much closer to true fitness. Yeah, this totally beats chasing stock investments or trying to find the nonexistent end of the housing market rainbow.

My treadmill beeps. It slows down and then stops with a sloughing sound. I almost forget to snap a photo of the distance I ran and climb back onto the machine even after it has stopped to take a quick selfie. After posting it, I refresh the feed several times in quick succession just to make sure everything looks good and to see who will be the first to comment.

Back in my room again, it feels like my legs are still running even when I sit still. Now that I've completed today's upload and have received enough "likes," I can finally, finally lie down and be at peace. I'm sure I'll fall asleep immediately tonight, and yet, even as I drift toward sleep, the little red video app icon on my phone beckons me like a fragrant, red rose.

"The number one reason you won't escape the rat race, and will continue living life as a wage slave."
"Still waiting to buy your first home? Follow these tips or regret it later!"
"Predictions: what uncertain financial markets could have in store for your stock portfolio."
"Social distancing at work: follow these five simple steps!"
"How to easily identify a sociopath in your social circle."

As I scroll down, new video recommendations lie in wait like so many pieces of cheese on so many rat traps devised especially for me to trigger. I remember pressing some sort of button to deny access to my personal information when I downloaded the app, but guess it does little to stop the algorithm from reading me like a book.

"Do you really think you'll be happy working for peanuts for the rest of your life? It will take ten lifetimes to become a millionaire on monthly wages like those! Remember to invest and diversify your assets! Invest, invest, invest! The difference between a rich man and a poor man is a little piece of paper. That, and the right mindset..."

A video recommendation pops up in my feed with a thumbnail that shows a familiar face I actually know from real-life. It's my old section head, Mr. Jung, who one day suddenly stood up at his desk and announced his resignation to the entire office in a solemn, but dignified voice. The next time everyone saw him, he had rebranded himself as "*Val-you*," the creator of "Poverty Therapy," a new video channel with over a million subscribers. He became a successful stockbroker guru and even sent a bottle of champagne to everyone in the office as a parting gift. His face used to be a sheet of heavy wrinkles that he carried every day to the office, but was now replaced with a bright, winning smile. How strange to see him shining back at me from the tiny screen on my phone in the darkness of my room.

"Hey, if you enjoyed this video, please, share, subscribe, and press the button to turn on notifications!"

I am suddenly jolted out of sleep by this last line of the video ringing in my ear. I guess I drifted off and let the video play to the end.

I close the app and put down my phone. Before shutting my eyes, I connect my phone to the long umbilical cord that keeps it on constant nocturnal life support. Good boy. I carefully place it beside me on the bed and fall asleep at last.

Should I Just Learn to Code?

My phone alarm blares in my ear. I let out a deep sigh that nobody but me will ever hear. Right. The only people that will ever come looking for me if something were to happen are my company and the bill collectors. I unplug my phone. At least you and I get to spend another day together. I give myself a clean shave and put on my pair of dress shoes with the backs worn out. They basically function as slippers because I'm too lazy to tie or untie the laces and simply step down on the heel. My door lock beeps its regular greeting to me as I head out the door and rush down the stairs. Its chipper tone seems to say, "Good morning! Seize the day today, Youngbaek!"

My commute takes place in the pastel streets of dawn. I walk back through the market towards the bus stop. The following eyes of the busy stall owners are like streetlights staring down at me. Emerging from the winding market, I can already see the traffic starting to pile up along the road. The bus stop is crowded with people wearing nearly the same outfit, regardless of gender—a variation of somber slacks, shirts, ties, and jackets. The bus will be here to pick us all up soon.

Beep, beep, beep-beep, beep... One by one the bus cards announce who is working today as we all climb into the bus. Crossing the bridge back over into Gangnam, the first rays of the sun greet those of us desperately trying to get in a few final moments of sleep. Peeking in through my eyelids, the rays seem to ask me, "Hey, did you sleep well!? No, it's not the sunset you're looking at, but the beginning of a brand new day!" I greet the day in my own special way by listlessly picking out a booger from the corner of my eye.

It's a shame I can't share this moment with the dozen or so friends that follow my account. Even though we'd likely have nothing to say to each other in real-life, I skim eagerly through the neon circles of their stories like popping so many pink balloons.

> "Days like this make me wish I could quit my job."
> "Yet another Tuesday! Go get 'em, everybody!"
> "On my way to work. Traffic's bad as usual."
> "Man, I have meetings all morning again today."

I can tell who made the last post about having meetings all day without even checking his username. It's Dongjoo Lee. He always makes the same humblebrag posts, and also happened to graduate from the same high school as me. Now he works as a programmer at M Corporation, the undisputed leader of the tech industry. Apparently, he found enough time in his busy schedule to take a photo of his computer monitor and carefully-positioned coffee cup and post it between his first and second meetings. Not a bad photo, though. I pay close attention to the persona he creates on social media because, at the end of last year, he received a performance bonus that was the size of my entire annual salary. It annoys me to no end that even though he did worse than I did in high school and graduated from a university that was a few levels below mine, he was still able to land a job as a programmer with M Corporation and seems to actually be happy with what he does.

The bus is nearing the stop in front of my company. I completely ignored the overhead announcement for the stop, but something deep in my subconscious automatically reacts, propelling me out of my seat, through the revolving doors, and into the office. The time is 08:57. I pray that I'll be able to put on a convincing appearance of working hard today.

"Good morning, Mr. Youngbaek, sir!"

It's Jungwoo. He arrived earlier than me and is already typing away at his keyboard. As expected, Jungwoo, just as bland and robotic as always, bows his daily greeting to me and diligently returns to his work. I hang my jacket on the back of my chair with a rustle. On the other side of my cubicle, my team leader clears his throat in a way that lets me know it was intended for me to hear.

I quietly take my seat and press the button on my computer tower to turn it on. For an instant, I see my face reflected in the dull gray monitor. It switches to a bright blue background. Unread emails and messages from the previous day pile up in my inbox like the wrinkles forming across my brow. Right, before any of this, a cup of coffee is what I need to start the day.

"Jungwoo, did you already have a coffee?"

"No, not yet."

"Want to get a cup with me?"

"Yes, sir."

We walk to the lounge area together, me holding my company-issued Tumbler with the logo half worn off. Coffee marks from what I drank yesterday still ring the inside. I press the button that makes the water come out cold and rinse it out until the rings disappear. Next, I take it over to the ice machine and place it under the dispenser. I press the button and the ice cubes fill up the tumbler with a tap-tapping sound.

"Uh, Youngbaek, sir?"

"Yes?"

"Do you... enjoy what you do?"

I extract my tumbler, now full to the brim with ice, and move it over to the hot coffee machine. The machine makes a loud noise as it grinds the beans into a fine powder.

"Well... it's just something we all have to do, right? Why do you ask? Getting tired of this place already?"

"No way. Not me. It's just... well, so many other people that started working for the company at the same time as me are quitting these days."

"I see. Well, think of it like this. Maybe they're just moving on to greener pastures."

The coffee machine makes a low, mechanical bubbling noise as it pours hot espresso over the ice in my Tumbler. Jungwoo reminds me of myself five years ago when I was around his age and just joined the company. Keep it together, young Jungwoo. The ice starts to crack and clatter as the scalding espresso melts it down.

"Sometimes I wish I would have become a software developer or something like that. That's what everyone else my age did. Now they're making a killing."

Whenever Jungwoo spouts out something naive like that, which doesn't fit the life of a company worker in the least bit, it reminds me of the sort of oblivious ignorance new employees bring with them to the job.

"Jungwoo, you shouldn't joke like that at work where people can hear you. But, if you ever do find a greener pasture, make sure you take me with you. Ha. Ha..."

"Ah-hem, aren't you two on the clock right now? Wouldn't want me to take this out of your working hours now, would you?"

This warning from our team leader, soft-spoken but resolute, muttered from across the room, hits our ears as though he were towering over us at the coffee machines.

"Right. Well, Jungwoo... good luck today and try to keep your head up. Um, good talking with you."

"Yes, erm... go get 'em, sir!"

It is now 09:13. I feel like I finished some meaningful work over the past thirteen minutes. I mean, many researchers consider water cooler talk to be good for office morale and productivity. At least, I'm pretty sure I read that somewhere.

Now it's time to roll up my sleeves and get to the real work. I zero in on my monitor and try to forget about the incessant notifications that keep popping up. Most are meaningless messages just to say thanks for our team's cooperation, emails I know I'll never respond to, or miscellaneous pop-ups that take up important screen real estate.

No matter how hard I try to move on from them, they keep coming like an endless game of Tetris. My fingers along the keyboard make the sound they usually make when furiously typing out a hurried reply. Next comes the sound of my landline ringing—it was the wrong number. Then I respond to a missed call from earlier and wait on the line for ages while no one answers. Finally, the sound of me slamming the phone back into its cradle rings out across the office and the brief silence that follows. Only then do I start to notice the other loud voices coming from the cluster of cubicles of the next team over. Slowly but surely, the tension level increases throughout the office. I overhear another phone conversation with what sounds like one of P Corporation's lowly subcontractors.

"I don't know. That's none of my business, just don't mess it up again, okay? What do we pay you for anyway? Don't you know I can get ten other subcontractors on the line to replace you before lunch!?"

More spells and curses being cast over phones. These are the techniques honed over generations that enable employees from big corporations like ours to yoke those beneath us and create something valuable out of nothing. My gaze zooms in on the minute hand of my desk clock, which seems to pause for a fraction of an instant, and I instinctively know that my current work sprint is nearly over. Five minutes to lunch and I fling the slippers I wear at my cubicle back under my desk, slip into my worn-out dress shoes and get ready to head out.

"Jungwoo, did you finish that thing I asked you to do the other day?"

It's generally a good habit to check in on your subordinates to keep them on their toes.

"I'll... I'll get that back to you right after lunch."

Something about Jungwoo's automatic and empty response fills me with a tinge of unease. I would have preferred him to offer up at least some kind of excuse instead of his straightforward reply. That's how it's done here.

Lunchtime is in full-swing. Both the team over from ours and the team over from theirs wait at the elevator doors to deliver us to the food on the basement floor below. There are chain restaurants and a cafeteria-style meal plan specifically for all the other office workers we share this building with. People in suits and ties descend in two single-file lines into the basement. The first option I see is a spicy stir-fried pork. My second pick is an omelet over rice. The two options are always vaguely the same from each day to the next, and I stand, as I always do, in front of the lines weighing which one to choose.

I bow to the kitchen staff and look for an empty seat. A smear of red ketchup smiles over the yellow of my egg. As always, nothing worth mentioning or laughing about happened at work so far today, so I sit there quietly. At least the kitchen staff had enough sense to bring a bit of humor into work today with their corny ketchup face. I slice through the omelet and rice, cutting it in half.

- *"Hey, have any dinner plans tonight?"*

The text message I've been waiting for arrives in my inbox right as I'm about to really dig in.

Dongjoo, my old highschool buddy over at M Corporation, has been bragging all morning about how busy he is being a programmer. His message hints that we should go out for dinner and drinks tonight.

- *"Drinks on you?"*
- *"Gangnam Station at seven. See you there?"*
- *"I'm in. How about inviting Inyoung?"*
- *"Did you check if he has time?"*
- *"Why wouldn't he? He was still a civil servant last time I checked. Plus it's not like he's dating anyone. He better have time."*

I have to remember to ask Dongjoo not to tag me in whatever he posts about dinner later on. I don't want my life broadcast on his feed for everyone to see.

It's dark tonight. Dinner and drinks. I feel the cold run through me and think about how I probably should have worn another layer. We go to the restaurant that I picked and as we take our seats, Inyoung is the first to start up a conversation.

"So, how have you two been holding up?"

Inyoung Choi also graduated from the same high school as us, then landed a job as a state-certified civil servant, which has always been the most highly-prized profession in Korea due to the fact that it offers both a stable future and almost never requires you to work overtime. People spend their entire youth trying to pass the state exam to land one of these coveted positions. So, in my opinion and in the estimation of virtually everyone else, Inyoung was a champion. Ever since securing his position even the way he talked sort of changed. Now he orated what he said like some sort of mythic hero returned from a long and desperate journey.

"It must have been real tough for you to make your way all the way from M Corporation down here just to see us. Well done."

"Not at all. All the best companies—and therefore restaurants, are in this neighborhood, isn't that right? Plus, I haven't seen either of you in ages. Anyway, I'm starving. How about barbecue? Don't worry, tonight's on me, fellas."

I can't help but chuckle at the sight of Dongjoo already starting to flex like he's some upper-level manager just because he's a fancy programmer now. In reality, I know that the ink on his employment contract is barely even dry yet. I'm the one that graduated from the best university in the country several years before you, you little punk.

"Three servings of pork belly over here, please!"

I order with the confidence of someone that is a regular here. After all, this restaurant is closest to P Corporation, where I work. It's on my turf. I select a few well-done pieces of meat from the grill, pick up some veggies along the way, and scoop a spoonful of rice. About to shove it all into my mouth, Dongjoo suddenly interrupts.

"So, are either of you ready to switch jobs yet? I'm not so sure about mine anymore..."

My heaping spoonful entirely misses my mouth and falls to the table. I mean, there's just no way Dongjoo can't be happy about his stellar new job. From his contract to his salary, he has the best benefits, plus a great healthcare plan to top it off. He was even offered stock options for Christ's sake! Inyoung plays along with this outrageous flex on the part of Dongjoo by offering him a few boilerplate words of encouragement. This is simply what successful people like us talk about when we meet over a hot grill.

"Yeah, but where would people with useless majors like us go?"

"You know, you could learn to code too, Inyoung. Want me to teach you sometime?"

Oh, look at Dongjoo patronizing us. What a cool guy.

"I'm good. But what about you, Youngbaek? You went to that fancy university. Wouldn't you make more doing sales or something?"

*

First-Place Award, Youngbaek Kim. The above child is awarded top honors at the elementary school philosophy debate competition...

Ever since I was young, I thought the reason I was born on this good, green earth was to live out my years dedicated to the pursuit of knowledge. When my high school homeroom teacher refused to write me a recommendation letter for anything except medical school or to become a lawyer, it only reaffirmed my desire to leave my mark as a brilliant academic rather than what everyone else thought I should be. At that age, I was willing to sacrifice a higher paycheck and go against the deeply ingrained belief that doctors and lawyers were the only two worthwhile professions.

"Youngbaek. Please, come to the front and solve this equation."

Picked again. I sat there with my arms crossed at the third desk from the left in the back of the class. I put on a practiced expression to let the others know I was worried about solving it, even though I already had the answer. If I didn't pretend like it was hard, who knows? Maybe I would be picked again next time and the next time after that.

The sound of chalk against the blackboard broke the silence. Eleventh grade me etching out the answer like raindrops falling on a roof. Tap, tap, tap. One by one, I arranged the formulas that I had memorized into neat little rows. The chalk spoke for me. Everyone sat at their desks mesmerized. The chalk let everyone know that the way to solve this particular equation was "Just. Like. This..." Then, with a final flourish, I showed how the answer was, of course, the number four. My cram school teacher gave me a quick nod of assurance.

"Look, everyone."

He made a sharp inhalation and let out a sigh, standing there in front of the blackboard. Then he slowly turned around and looked sternly at us students.

"If you all try to solve this equation by taking as many steps as Youngbaek did just now, none of you will ever be able to finish the entrance exam in time. Each minute is precious. That is what you should all take from this."

I imagined how I felt was exactly what it would be like to watch a famous painting be destroyed. My ears started to burn and turned red.

"You see, the way that you try to solve the problem doesn't matter one bit. It's all about the answer!"

I just barely made out the sound of a piece of mechanical pencil lead snapping somewhere behind me. Even the students sitting at the back, who were smiling and horsing around until now, were dead silent. My chin suddenly felt heavy and I couldn't seem to lift it.

"Do you know what will happen if you try to solve an equation like this when you take the exam for real? You only have one year left. And while everyone else your age is living it up at the top universities, you'll be stuck spending another grueling year at this cram school until you can answer the questions faster. Your entire life depends on the scores you'll get that day. Do you understand that, Youngbaek?"

A few years later, the yard of my high school was still covered in snow as I plodded through it. The world hadn't changed as much as I thought it would as I steadily approached my final and most life-changing senior year. I saw a boy dragging his feet and doodling something on a wall that the whole school would eventually read. He stopped scribbling to kick an errant ball back to the middle of the field. The other students walked up the stairs and down the hallway carrying the same textbook under their arms.

Elegant Math: Special Lecture Series

They were carrying their books under their arms in the manner our cram school teacher taught us was the "correct" way to carry them. The first word in the title, "Elegant," was written in big, bold letters at the top of the book. To my high school mind, there was something about that word and the font they chose for the cover that seemed to guarantee you would get a perfect score on the college entrance exam, so long as you could memorize its contents. Dogeared textbooks, stiff new writing pads, and workbooks covered from top to bottom in yellow highlighter were always carried with the front cover facing outward, so they could be visible to anyone who cared to look. My schoolmates and I recited the abbreviations of our favorite universities like the incantations of powerful incantations.

In the corner of the classroom, my classmates and I stood over a desk with a list of universities on it debating our chances. There were some we wouldn't go to even if they paid us to, while others would require us to study a whole extra year even just to have a chance at getting in. We could be divided into those of us who the teachers believed would do well, and therefore gave extra attention to, and those who had little hope and were simply left to their own devices. The ones that got left behind spent their senior year with a certain resigned sense of relief and were usually content to munch on snacks in the school cafeteria and waste away the time.

I was inside a cold, cluttered teacher's room. I could hear the voices of my classmates through a thin partition that served as a wall to divide the office. I could imagine them all sitting the same way, shoulders hunched, heads bowed, waiting to talk with our homeroom teacher. One at a time, our teacher called us up and did everything he could to persuade us away from our dreams, emphasizing that people often have to put aside personal preference and aspirations to prioritize entry into prestigious universities. This part was crucial and he repeated it often. One student, overwhelmed by what he heard, began to sob, his head bowed between his shoulders. Still shaking his head at the student, our homeroom teacher left the room for a smoke break. I sat there knowing that my turn was next.

"So, have you changed your mind yet?"

My homeroom teacher always started our conversations with this question.

"I still want to study philosophy of science."

"But why? With grades like yours, you could easily apply for a second-rate medical school, maybe somewhere outside the city that's more affordable. Why are you so stuck on this philosophy stuff?"

"Because I like it. Science is about the underlying structure that explains... well everything."

"I... see..."

I could already tell what words would form on his lips as he stared at me and let out a deep sigh.

"Philosophy of science, huh? You know, it's hard enough to make ends meet in this country of ours with any kind of degree at all, let alone something impractical like that. It's about time you wake up and smell the coffee, young man."

*

"Listen, Youngbaek. I got a message from this new recruitment service. What was it called... Quantum Jump or something?"

Quantum Jump... in my mind, the name brings up an image of the quantization of the energy of electrons. Something I remember from a physics book I saw once. I bet Dongjoo, sitting across the table from me, has never even heard of Schrödinger's equation before.

"Don't you want to switch companies yet, Youngbaek?"

A piece of meat scalds my tongue. I cough to disguise the faux pas.

"I like where I'm at now. Ha. Ha... Yeah, I think it suits me just fine. Plus, I happen to be pretty decent at what I do, thank you."

"Well, I did hear a rumor that P Corporation is giving out 300% performance bonuses this quarter. Let's see if your tune changes after you get that fat bonus. I mean, you've got the potential to work anywhere you want."

Dongjoo must have misheard. The bonus we were promised was a flat $3K, not 300% of our paycheck. It's a sad but important detail to have to refute, still, I don't even bother. I fixate on how much sadder it will be if they expect me to pay the bill on account of that misinformation. I choose to say nothing at all and just sit there and smile.

"Ha. Ha. I guess I'll have to think about it, then. By the way, do they even look at your academic background if you apply somewhere as a programmer?"

"No, academics don't matter at all. Ha! It's all about skills."

Inyoung spits out a small fragment of bone that was hidden in a piece of barbecue onto the table and quickly wraps it in a napkin.

"Really? They must at least consider what school you went to though?"

"I'm telling you, they don't care about your diploma at all. It's all about what you can do. What, do you think every company merely looks at what university you went to like yours does?"

Dongjoo lets out a satisfied sigh and then drains his cup.

"What's wrong with my company? Don't look down on me like

that."

"Who says I'm looking down on you? I'm just telling the truth."

I reach across the table and my cup of cold water spills a bit over the grill, causing steam to rise up and then dissipate. Inyoung, who up until now has been sitting quietly and turning the meat, decides to pitch in.

"Hey, you two. Come on. Let's just eat. I mean, we're all wage slaves here anyway, right?"

"Whatever. Should we ask them to refill these side dishes?"

"Fine by me."

My student ID. Where did it go? Where did I put that symbol of pride? What happened to that feeling I used to get when I casually mentioned what school I went to? It's helped me through so many situations. And, for that matter, where did the old, pathetic Dongjoo Lee go? The one so jealous I got into a better school than him that he would squirm to try and avoid the topic or change the subject as best he could. Where did I put my student ID? The fullness I feel from all the meat we just ate only makes me more keenly aware of a deeper hunger within me. Dongjoo, looking strong and self-assured, comes back with a powerful retort.

"So, are you two ready for the second round, or what?"

"I'm too tired to go to a bar tonight. What about you, Inyoung?"

"Count me out. How are you getting home, anyway?"

"Come on, I came all the way over here to see you two and you're calling it quits already?"

Dongjoo loudly broadcasts his disappointment. It's all a part of his flex, he must really want to go home too.

"Next time, then. We'll make plans in advance. Youngbaek, you take the subway, right?"
"You guys go ahead. I'll take the bus by myself."
"All right, see you, then."
As soon as I'm back in the darkness of my room, I kick off my shoes and turn on the light. The smell of grilled pork on my clothes spreads throughout my entire tiny space. I'm feeling too full to lie down. I sit down at my desk and press the button to turn on my computer with the tip of my big toe. The same video platform greets me across my screen. I remember as a child having to tap the keyboard so carefully to keep my parents from knowing I was using it. I enter the following search with the same furtive movements.

Search: how to be a programmer

I guess there are a lot of people trying to get into coding these days. I'm probably just one of thousands of gazelles out there wandering the Sahara Desert to the video creators who upload the thumbnails I rapidly scroll through. Easy prey. Still, I'm not delusional enough to fall for the loftier claims like, "Become a programmer in minutes after watching this single video!" But, I do get sucked into watching the one that comes after it: "The three types of people that should never get into programming."

The welcome screen of a coding program I installed with great difficulty greets me like a night sky. A few unreachable stars shine off in the darkness. Without really knowing anything about their meaning, I recite the terms I learn aloud as though memorizing multiplication tables. For no reason at all, I tap extra loudly on the keyboard. Somehow it makes me feel like I'm working harder.

```
#include <stdio.h>
int main()
{
    printf("Hello World!");
    return 0;
}
```

Me, Youngbaek Kim, a man of infinite promise and potential in the prime of his youth. A rising star who will one day drink the sky itself! I used to wish that I would contribute something meaningful and lasting to the world. I thought I would become a brilliant physicist capable of taming the fires of Prometheus. Yes, I once dreamed of fighting it out on the frontlines of human knowledge. I would lift the flame and smile to myself, thinking of the great lineage of scientists before me who also handled the torch of progress.

Now I'm just a thirty-two-year-old cog in the wheels of P Corporation, pushing the same revolving door every day like Sisyphus. I have a headache. It's about time to sleep. I give up coding for the night. I start to steel myself against the next day before me. A day of running around and trying to shield myself from the constant requests and demands of my seniors or–even worse–another mandatory after-hour work party.

The Bridle

"Got my incentive pay today! :)"

Sitting in front of my civil complaint desk at the local community center, head slumped down between my shoulders, I count out the bonus pay Youngbaek posted on his social media one zero at a time. Storm clouds gather over what should be the joy of his first payday since taking this new position. Good for you, Youngbaek. I can't believe office workers make 300% of their yearly salary in a single bonus check.

A delivery guy drops off a huge box by the door of the community center. It's a bundle of dozens of rice cakes wrapped in individual plastic baggies in a large paper box. A small note is attached to each of the rice cakes. "Enjoy this small token of my appreciation and thank you for your continued support!" I take one of the cakes into my hand and stand up from my desk. The first one will go to the most influential person in the building, and therefore for my career. Yes, this rice cake has the head of the department's name on it.

"Hello, sir. This is for you. Please take it as a token of my appreciation!"

"A rice cake? Inyoung, you shouldn't have..."

"Well, I got my first paycheck today since moving to this assignment, so I thought I would spend it on the team. Ha. Ha..."

"I guess it's the mark of an experienced government worker like yourself. Looking after your superiors like this is a sign of sound upbringing. Fine work, Inyoung, as always. Take care and if there's anything you have any questions about, feel free to ask me any time."

Our section chief's expression brightens when I hand over the rice cake—a small bit of my first paycheck gone, just like that.

"Thank you, sir. I appreciate your support!"

Phew. I practically had to turn my wallet upside down and shake it to afford these rice cakes. They're more expensive than they look! But, I guess it's a decent investment to avoid spending the next year in an uncomfortable work environment. Every little thing that greases the wheels in this line of work counts. Hopefully, this small gesture will go a long way... and maybe even work towards getting me my next promotion.

The doors to the civil complaint office open at nine. On the hour, an elderly man pushes the doors open and walks straight over to where I'm seated. And, here we go! Remember, friendly responses make happy citizens. You got this.

"Hello, sir. What brings you here today?"

"Oh, I'm here to submit one of those... those... whatchamacallits."

I'm a fourth-year civil servant. A request like this is no sweat.

"Sorry, but what exactly did you say you are here for today, sir?"

"You know... that thing. What was it, again? Some kind of utility voucher?"

I'm not sure exactly what he's talking about. My gut tells me that figuring out this case will require some extra backup.

"I see, sir. Well, please just wait a moment and I'll be right back with you."

I swivel my chair over and whisper to the other officer sitting beside me.

"Excuse me, um... team manager?"

"What is it?"

"Can you help me figure out how to settle an application for a utility voucher?"

"Oh, well that's not within the scope of my responsibilities. I'm afraid you'll have to find someone else to help you."

"I see. Well, thanks anyway. Sorry for bothering you."

What are the odds? On the same day I handed him my little token of gratitude, I already need the section chief's help. I should kick myself for having been so hesitant to press the "buy" button for my hefty online rice cake purchase. It looks like my investment is going to pay off immediately. I tiptoe over to the section chief's desk.

"Excuse me, chief, but I have a question."

He simply stares back at me blankly and then adjusts his glasses. I take this as a cue to go ahead.

"Could you tell me how to submit an application for a utility voucher?"

"Ah-hem..."

My heart starts to pound. His response lets me know that I've somehow messed up by bringing this to his attention. The voice of the senior citizen taking his complaint to the other sections gets louder and travels across the room to where we're standing.

"I mean, come on... Are you really bringing such a trivial matter to my desk? This is something you should be able to solve on your own in five minutes. Didn't you search for how to do it?"

My team manager, who only just a moment ago completely refused my plea for help, rushes over to assist the elderly man. Before he starts processing the application, he takes one meaningful look at me clearly relaying that I owe him one for this.

"Oh, hello sir. Allow me to help you with that. It should only take a moment."

I try my best to memorize the process, watching the movements of the mouse from over my team manager's shoulder. You click there, then there... then check that box there. I have to give up. Trying to remember all the steps at this speed is impossible and he doesn't appear to be slowing down at all for my benefit. I look down at my clumsy hands and feet, while I stand awkwardly by as my work is done for me. I look up at one of the posters attached to the wall next to our desks.

Please refrain from swearing at or assaulting public officials.

Failure to do so may include a fine and is punishable by law. Kindly remember that civil servants are people too, with families of their own

Satisfied, the senior citizen opens the door and walks back out. I rotate my entire body toward my team manager and the section chief, ready to face what I know will come next.

"Well, that's that."

I feel empty. I started the day with such purpose and this is how I am rewarded. Everyone always praises the government for being the most forward-thinking with regard to workplace culture, but when it comes down to it, it's still every man for himself.

"Hey. Yeah, it's been a while. Oh yeah? Well, how have you been? I see, I see..."

The section chief talks loudly on the phone.

"Yeah, yeah. By the way, how is that new person you hired working out for you?"

These last words hit my ears like lightning. A cold sweat starts to run down my back.

"I mean, I've watched the same videos everybody else has about these new Gen Z workers. Heck, we even had that training session a while back, didn't we? Anyway, we've got one over here that's way too free-spirited. Yeah. Yeah, no. I mean, he knows nothing outside of himself. Yeah, absolutely no self-awareness. Back in the day, there was no on-job training. I mean, are we supposed to hold these kids by the hand and teach them everything? I know! Right, right..."

My eyes are wide open, but I can't see anything in front of me.

It's like I'm watching the world through the back of my head, where somewhere our section chief is sitting and complaining about me. The rest of the rice cakes on my desk stare back at me. It's almost like they're smiling. *Thank you for your continued support!* A new message pops up on my monitor. One unread document requires my urgent attention.

You Have Been Assigned a New Task:
Assume Any Additional Responsibilities Pertaining to the Energy Voucher Management

I return home after drinks and barbeque with my old high school buddies in the private sector. Talk of the 300% incentive pay certain companies are offering is still ringing in my ears. A sort of damp, oily smell envelops me, and I can still feel little pieces of meat caught uncomfortably in between my teeth. I am suddenly self-conscious of my non-designer brand clothes and shoes.

At my age, I should have a thick wallet instead of this waistline. A constant stream of people gets sucked into the entrance of the subway station in front of me. I shuffle my way to the back of the line of people going in.

It's already been two years since I started working at what everyone else thinks is the best job in the world. At that time, getting a position in the government, even starting out as a lowly intern like

I did, was so competitive that the acceptance rate was one in two hundred. Here, standing in line to go down into the subway station, where the footprints of my own youth are buried somewhere deep beneath the tiles and stairs, I encounter young people still in their P.E. clothes with backpacks and stacks of books tucked under their arms.

<Elegant Employment: Special Lecture>
<Power Potential: Advanced Calculus Operations>
<Test-prep: Follow these Simple Instructions and Achieve Your Dreams!>

While cram school textbooks are physically light enough to be held under one arm, the anguish and torment they cause results in students having to carry them with both hands, their bodies bent forward at a worry-inducing angle. I remember because I used to be like that too. As each student passes by, I glower at the books they carry which are now, thankfully, no longer any of my business. They no longer have any power over me or the narrative I live in. I squeeze my eyes shut. No, my story is today about the balance left in my bankbook at the end of this endless flight of stairs. I trudge down and into the subway.

Deposit: $3,521.67
Withdrawal: $2,000 (Savings Account)
Balance: $1,521.67

My paycheck was like a gently floating bird impaled by the arrow of my monthly rent. In order to work where I was assigned, I had to move to the very center of the city, the most expensive part of the already-expensive metropolis that is Seoul. To live in a place like this, you have to absorb an onslaught of arrows, with your paycheck and ultimately your body. I see a person running through the subway to catch the train before the doors shut in their face. A common sight.

"Please stand back, the safety doors are now closing."

The young students getting on the strain squeeze through gaps between bodies. They try to find a spot big enough to take out their phone and study. The ones that find enough room start memorizing as many English words as they can. It isn't easy. There was a time when I spent every morning feeling like I was walking the same tightrope they are now walking. The only thing is, I used to believe that by the end of the rope, I would be able to climb down safely. Now, I spent a third of my salary buying what were essentially rice cake bribes for my boss and colleagues.

"Do you want to work far away or close to Seoul? Become a first-rate marriable candidate on your way to becoming a civil servant. There is no employment quite as **Elegant** as this!"

This ad, splayed across the walls of the subway, seems to follow me wherever I go, like the moon in a starless sky. The jingle of the ad hits my ears in between train arrival announcements, *"Do you want to work far away or close to Seoul?"* Seoul has everything to offer. Even living just a few miles outside of its center makes it that much more difficult to meet friends and find a potential mate.

Balance: $921.67

I can't help but check my balance every now and then because I'm still not used to receiving the amount I get from my monthly paycheck.

Four years ago, I promised myself I would give it my all. I practically lived at school studying for the college entrance exam in the final years of my youth. If you pass, you can do whatever you want! You'll have plenty of time to think about all the things you'll do after you make it! Is what everyone around me constantly reminded me every step of the way. I used to believe it too.

"Hey, now. Are you daydreaming?"

The most sought-after teacher in the Elegant Employment cram school franchise, Ms. Sora Kim, tapped her microphone and took a drink from her glass of water, preparing for the lecture she was about to give.

"Now, back to the lesson…"

Every student in the class turned their head to look in my direction. Each eye aimed at me was piercing.

"Excuse me. I apologize."

"Oh, nothing to be sorry about. You seem like you've got at least basic etiquette down, so you'll probably make it out all right!"

A student set a drink down on her podium and bowed as he scurried away. She was about to start.

"Ah-hem. Thank you for the drink, by the way."

Always there to greet us as we entered with her warm, welcoming smile, this educator, no this purveyor of the secrets to employment-had only the deepest regard for her pupils, even more so than the teachers at regular public schools who were just there to get a paycheck and leave, not top professionals in their field like her. When the class grew sleepy during a lecture, she would sometimes go off on a fascinating tangent from her own life, which were usually easier to remember than the lessons themselves. And before beginning a lecture, she always started with a dramatic pause.

"... First, I know that you are all going through a tough time. I know how much pressure you are under to succeed at this age. Young people always talk about how hard it is, but in all my sixty years, this is probably the most difficult job market I've ever seen. It wasn't even this bad during the economic crash of the 1990s. At least people had something to hope for back then..."

I noticed the face of the student beside me had turned yellow. Perhaps he hadn't seen the sun in a few days. His eyes were bloodshot. I contemplated whether that could be caused by subsisting on a meager diet of steamed rice, like I did. We all spent many late nights over a microwaveable container of rice and a can of tuna fish.

"What, then, can we do about it? The reality of the matter isn't an easy pill to swallow. The entire nation is burdened by the current financial climate, young people chiefly among them. Sometimes I even wonder whether I'm qualified to stand up here and lecture you at all. The world has changed so much. But, we have to push onward. You have to take one step farther than those sitting beside you. Pass the exam, become the pride of your parents, stand tall and straight among your peers, and, of course, find a suitable spouse to marry."

That is the reason why I studied for two straight years while eating half-cooked rice with nothing but canned tuna to wash it down with. *Do you want to work far away or close to Seoul?* I remembered these words haunting me even on the day I finally took my exams. I've had to listen to the words of that ad all the way to my current employment. Still, people say you feel a sense of relief when you pass the peak and come down the other side of the mountain. I just wish someone would have told me that it would be more like an elevator than a mountain. And that I would be one of the last ones to get on... plummeting straight down. The constant fluctuations of my bank account, like a perplexing computer error–or a persistent rock I can't seem to get out of my non-designer shoes–poke at the soles of my feet all the way home.

"I'm home."

"Is that you, Inyoung? How was work?"

"Same as always... anything to eat?"

"Don't you think it's time you came home to a wife that cooks for you instead of me?"

"Mom!"

"Sorry, you must be so tired of me saying the same old thing..."

"It's not like I'm not trying, Mom."

"Everything in its own time. Don't worry too much about whether you're ready to get married or not and just meet someone already. Sometimes it's fun to save up little by little, one step at a time."

Who doesn't want to date? But it's completely useless to try to talk to your parents about the decline in real income or that fact the problem of meeting someone is only compounded by the increasing gender imbalance caused by things like abortion or due to the historical preference for sons over daughters that my mom's generation very much believed in. It's people your age that got us here in the first place! Whatever, when you still live with your parents, marriage is just a conversation you have to have, I guess.

"It's all because young people these days are so selfish. Back in my time, we never took anything for granted and we had absolutely nothing! Now everyone walks around with their stomachs so full, they can only focus on whatever it is that they want. I'm telling you, our country is doomed. Yet, compared to how I lived, your generation is living in opulence. In a golden age..."

This point that my mother often recites only leads to one of my main positions on the matter: that other people's parents always pay for their kids' down payments when they lease their first homes. Everyone else gets plenty of support from their parents when they get married, so where is mine? I mean, how many grandchildren does she expect me to have based on the measly amount she may or may not be able to pitch in against the hundreds of thousands it costs to get married and have kids in a city like Seoul?

"So, are you going to go out and meet a nice girl next week, then?"

"Mom, I told you I'd take care of it myself...."

*

On an idyllic weekend afternoon, I leave home with my head held high. On this day, I'll meet the girl a friend has been trying to set me up with on a blind date with. According to our mutual acquaintance, she is *the* number one most eligible candidate. I all but dance to the rhythm that my shoes make going down the subway stairs today.

As a train passes by on the opposite side of the tunnel, I watch the people sitting through the window. Then I take a look at myself in the reflection and notice I look way better than I usually do. My body sways a bit as I hang onto the subway handle, dressed in a kind of drab sprezzatura. Four more stops until I arrive where we agreed to meet. I'd better start planning the flow of our conversation. Did you take the bus or subway? What did you say you did for work again? Really, and what do you do after-hours? On the weekends? I happened to see your profile picture, and... do you like traveling? Really? I do too! I've been through this sort of thing so many times, I've made it out with more than just a bruised ego–by this point, I've committed the script to memory.

As I exit the subway, my eyes are confronted by a cold blast as I look up to see the clear sky above me. A roughly-hewn stone wall stretches upward toward the pure blue expanse. Cherry blossom branches sway in the wind. A pair of young people sit arm-in-arm under the shade of a tree. They face one another under a heavy bough of blossoms in a timeless scene that looks as though it might really last forever.

I arrive thirty minutes early at the cafe where we said we'd meet. I order a cup of coffee filled to the brim with ice, stir my drink around with a straw, and review the script that is about to unfold.

"Hello!"

A bouquet of yellow freesias stands brightly in a corner of the coffee shop's wood tones. As she walks in, I get up from my seat and bow politely to her.

"Well, hello!"

In the middle of her greeting, she glances down at her wristwatch.

"Please, you don't have to stand for me. You're so early... how um, how did you get here?"

A granite pillar seems to fall right on the middle of my chest. I know that navigating the awkwardness that can stem from a seemingly simple question like this will be no simple feat. It only takes me a fraction of an instant to identify her angle here. This is her attempt to indirectly ask whether I own my own car or not.

"Oh, I came here by subway. Don't you just love how accessible Seoul is?"

Right, it's perfectly reasonable that I'm not at the stage where I can afford a car, the insurance, the automobile tax, and pay for maintenance yet. Surely she understands that.

"Oh, then did you leave your car at home or something?"

"No, I actually don't own a car of my own. Who needs one?"

At least I've made it clear that I don't have a car. I'm being forthright, right? However, my stomach suddenly feels tied up in knots, and I pay the psychological toll for this admission, feeling on the backfoot as a cold sweat forms on my forehead.

"Oh, where do you live, then?"

"I live pretty near the center of Seoul. What about you, do you have your own place?" Completely ignoring my question, she forges on:

"Really? So, do you lease or rent?"

"Oh, ha. I um... asked you first."

"I live in Gangnam. So, do you lease, then?"

"Yes, I lease. Or, rather, my parents do. I still live with them"

"You're not looking for a spouse that also works, are you?"

"Oh, um... Ha. Ha..."

What I really want to say is that I'm looking for a partner. I don't know how many times I've had to go through this sort of interrogation since I entered my thirties, but I'm suddenly so, so tired of it.

"Look, let's just stop here."

It just came out of me.

"Excuse me?!"

"I mean, I'm sure you'll meet someone nice someday. Something came up. Let's just split the bill and go our separate ways."

"Wait, shouldn't you pay for it then?"

"... Excuse me?"

"I guess that people in your position all act like this then?"

I pause to think about just what I did wrong to our mutual friend who tried to set me up with this person. Didn't I buy her coffee the last time we met? Why would she introduce me to someone like her put me through this?

"Can I ask you one more thing? Are you satisfied with your simple desk job?"

"Are you done talking?"

"Your job probably makes you do a ton of over-time, isn't that right? I bet it doesn't even come with any parental leave. *Tsk tsk...* I'm surprised you could even find time in your schedule to come all the way over here for this little date of ours. I mean, if you were better looking then I'd probably be more patient with you, but since you look the way you do..."

A five-dollar bill is flung into the air and then wafts down to the table in front of me. She bumps into the table as she gets up and turns around to leave. In this game, there are no winners, only losers. The hairstyle and clothing I put so much work into over the weekend now just feel pathetic to me. Just where did I go wrong? Was it actually the moment I took the civil service entrance exam? Or because I was born a simple, round pebble on the beach of life instead of a beautiful, geometrical gem? I fold the five-dollar note and stick it in my wallet. Then place the wallet in my jacket pocket, next to my heart.

I get up and walk out of this interrogation room. An air of relief hits me as I feel the cool breeze against my forehead again. Everywhere I look are pairs of lovebirds carousing the weekend streets. I go into a restaurant by myself and order a bowl of fish roe over rice. I squat down on a stool, then toss my phone over to one corner of the table set for one person.

"Phew..."

I feel dazed. All of my anticipation and preparation for the day flows out of me with that single sigh. I consciously try to straighten my back and shoulders as I sit waiting for the simple relief of a meal.

The bowl of rice and roe is placed in front of me. I sit there like a student studying in a library, surrounded by others but utterly alone, distant, unreachable. The rice makes a crackling sound as it continues to cook in the earthenware bowl. I use my spoon to scoop up a heart-shaped portion of rice speckled with tiny pink fish eggs. Then I jam it back down into the bowl and mix it all together. My expectations and frustrations combine with the steam coming from the bowl. The first spoonful is almost suffocatingly hot. I clear my throat loudly. Tears well up in my eyes.

My food starts to cool down. My heart, which only this morning was boiling over with hope and anticipation, becomes lukewarm. Trickles of sweat stream down my forehead. I swish around the eggs and rice in my mouth with a gulp of cold water and wash it all down.

"Thank you and enjoy your evening!"

The cashier's words are filled with such positive energy and an indomitable spirit that I don't even begin to try to match their tone. I don't have the energy to reply and merely incline my head a bit as I walk out the door.

Enveloped in the oily smell of the restaurant, I bring its scent with me out into the open air. The sun is still shining from about the same angle. Clouds wistfully float across the blue sky. Cherry blossoms blown by the wind scatter along the pavement like so many failed attempts at love. Pairs of young people, who have come all this way here to see the final bloom of spring, snap pointless photos under heavy-laden boughs.

Trying to trick myself back into believing that I'm too busy to be upset, as busy as Wonderland's white rabbit, in fact I pull my phone from my pocket. Youngbaek and Dongjoo are still arguing about the same old mundane topics in our group chat. Youngbaek's profile picture shows a pair of roses that seem to hint, but in a completely obvious way, that he might be about to finally tie the knot with his girlfriend. I mean, what appears to be a diamond ring worth at least $5K is right there in the middle of the photo. No need to rush. The sun is still out. My youth has yet to fall into the shadow of the evening. A banner ad passes across the top of the messaging app I use.

Stuck spending another spring solo?
Meet the top 1% of sexy singles.
Offer ends soon!

The Mistake

Dear Mr. Dongjoo Lee, We are pleased to inform you that you have passed the required competency test for M Corporation. The date of your interview will be announced at a later date. Please use the remaining time to prepare, and on behalf of the entire team, we wish you the best of luck.

Application number: 51012202

That's it. I got through to the second round. Only the final inter- view with M Corporation was left. Truth be told, having to take the competency test remotely was like watching a flickering lantern from afar and just praying it wouldn't go out. I spent the whole time wringing my hands worried that a clueless family member might come home and want to use the internet or someone would ring the doorbell and interrupt me during this most critical of moments. That's why I removed the batteries from the electronic door lock so that no one could enter and disturb me, just in case.

Many consider M Corporation to be the number one company in Korea. Its logo is emblazoned in its trademark silver and green.

I can already imagine handing out one of their brilliantly-colored business cards with my name on it.

"Hi, my name is Dongjoo, a programmer at M Corporation." This fantasy plays itself out over and over in the privacy of my empty house as I listen to my own voice echoing off the sur- rounding walls. I roll the battery from the door lock in my fingertips. "Yes, I do work for M Corporation. So, can I leave my card with you and touch bases later?"

What was the right way to exchange a business card? Are you supposed to offer them yours first? Or ask for theirs first?

"May I have one of your business cards, please?"

I need to calm down a little. To get my own business card from M Corporation in the first place, I still have to finish one last interview. It will take place next month and then I can just sit back and wait for the good news. Still, I can't help myself as a jolt of electricity seems to shoot down my spine and run through my hand as I yank my phone from my pocket and immediately start texting.

- *"LOL, I passed the first interview!"*
- *"Wow! We are so proud of you, son."*

I can already imagine myself grinning with my new colleagues while sipping a hot cup of coffee. I can't wait to leave scalding replies on the posts of people from other companies in SCR33N. Even though I'm elated to even have a chance to work somewhere like M Corporation, at the same time, I can already see myself posting about all the downfalls of working there, talking trash about my colleagues and supervisors. If I could, I'd shoot an arrow straight into the sun in defiant proclamation of my admission to this company. I really made it, and that justified all the cocky disdain and self-confidence that comes with it.

Yes, I too, will soon be a proud employee of M Corporation. To make sure I have enough energy for the day of my interview, I think I'll order an entire chicken and eat it all by myself. I order from one of the most expensive fried chicken places on my delivery app and exuberantly toss my phone onto the couch.

"Yes, sir! I'll get right on it. Certainly, you're the boss..."

My phone vibrates.

Snatching my phone with its scratched screen from the couch, I see a new message from Youngbaek.

- *"Hey, did you really get in? LOL!"*

Youngbaek Kim, an alumni from my high school. He graduated from a university that was slightly more prestigious than mine and has never let me live it down. Who even pays attention to that stuff, anyway? He acts like some sort of desperate monk greedily counting each step towards enlightenment. He was lucky to get in with P Corporation in the first place, which, I might point out, is the second-best company in Korea, ha! Still, he's been there a few years already so he's already an assistant manager. Youngbaek's smugness for landing that job always did annoy me...

- *"Yes, I got in. Ha! Would you look at that!"*

I reply to his text, grinding my teeth.

- *"But... you still have one more interview left, right?"*

I think to myself how the ink he signed his contract with is barely even dry yet. Who does he think he is? You have to laugh at a guy who already talks like he's the head of an entire department, even though he still doesn't have a clue.

- *"Yeah, but I've got it in the bag!"*
- *"LOL! Well, I'll be rooting for you. If you need any advice, just let me know. :)"*

The idea of writing him back telling him exactly how much I don't need his advice or any help from him for that matter passes my mind.

- *"What do you think they'll ask in the interview?"*

After messaging back and forth, he suddenly takes his sweet time to respond to my text. I figure he's doing it on purpose and have to shake my head at his pettiness. This is a new low, Youngbaek.

- "Oh, nothing too hard. They just want to make sure you're not too much of a weirdo."

- "Right. Got it."

- "Hey Dongjoo, you have a lot of time on your hands these days, right? How about you let me take you out to dinner to celebrate?"

Does everyone turn into this kind of person when they land a job at a company? I've heard that P Corporation brainwashes its new recruits as soon as they enter. Maybe their onboarding process teaches them how to be arrogant little pricks.

- "You know, I totally would... but I'm a bit tired today."

- "Come on, it's on me. I mean it! Don't make me call everyone up and make it a high school reunion."

Well, I think, it won't be that much longer that I can enjoy being unemployed, anyway. I'll wash my hands of this sort of petty mockery after I become a software developer at M Corporation.

It was a cold winter evening. The three of us sat around one of those circular tin tables with a pit in the middle that are the trademark of the kind of barbecue restaurants office workers frequent after a thirsty day at the office. It was Inyoung Choi, with his government position, Youngbaek Kim of P Corporation, and me, still unemployed, but only for the time being. We all graduated from the same high school. But I was still twenty-nine and this felt like the longest winter of my life. I had entire patches of hair missing from my head that had fallen out in clumps with each successive unsuccessful job application. Why was I the only one left without a job? What was supposed to be a fun table of drinking and eating, from my perspective, was divided between the employed and unemployed–between those with respectable, secure, and well-paying jobs, and those without.

"Cheer up, Dongjoo. I mean, any job is just being a slave to your boss."

"Yeah, dude. P Corporation is nothing special."

"So, what am I supposed to do? Starve to death for the rest of my life?"

"At least you have some semblance of a work-life balance, Inyoung. I mean, I'd work less and take it out of my paycheck, if they let me."

Work? Life? Balance?! Isn't work life? I mean... no work, no life... right?

"It's not like they let just anyone into positions like ours."

Back then, I was the same Dongjoo Lee who finally finished his bachelor's degree at the ripe age of twenty-seven. The same Dongjoo Lee who consistently failed to land a job two years after graduating. The same Dongjoo Lee who graduated from a university with close connections in the media industry that I should have been able to leverage. The same Dongjoo lee who still regrets the single, irrevocable mistake I made on the math section of my college entrance exam all those years ago. The same Dongjoo Lee who sat staring blankly at the cup in front of him because I was unsure of what expression to make at all.

"Look, Dongjoo. I'm sure you'll get there someday. I mean, look at me. I went to a worse college than you did, didn't I?"

That was exactly the kind of thing that somebody who already passed the civil service exam and landed a job would say.

"Yeah, man. You know I also messed up my grades in college big time."

Classic Youngbaek. What he failed to mention was how he also graduated from Sky University, one of the best, and was now working at P Corporation, the most well-known. What did he have to complain about? The ink on his employment contract was definitely still wet and here he was testing my nerves with snide remarks.

Several shots in and the surfaces of the green glass started to look like they were dripping tears down from their silver caps. I've never seen Soju do that before.

"Excuse me, can we have some water over here, please?"

I sat there drunkenly on my stool waiting for the server to come back with the water. A few weeks ago, in the beginning of November, a sudden cold snap hit that made me look back on my entire life. I'll be thirty soon and will have to draw another ring in the stump that is my age. I waited expectantly for the spring, only a few months away, with the hope that it would bring an end to my unemployment. It still felt too far away.

"I'm telling you! It's all because of that damn minus sign I misread on question number three!"

When the server came back, I poured the icy water into one of the small stainless-steel cups on the table. Sipping from the tiny cup, I waited drunkenly for anyone, even the empty green bottles, to ask me what's been bothering me lately to get it off my chest.

"Look, he's drunk. He's talking about that math problem again."

Piss off. I'm not drunk. Anyway, it doesn't matter to me what brand of suit you wear to a simple meeting with friends. Overdress much, Youngbaek? I didn't come here wearing my gym clothes to broadcast to the world that I don't have a job!

"No... really. If I had gotten that one question right, they would have let me into Sky, for sure."

"Come on, man... give it a break already."

"What did you say?"

I felt a familiar tingling sensation in the back of my head in the same spot where my sergeant used to hit me during my two-year mandatory military service.

"I said take it easy, dude!"

Hearing Youngbaek's tone, I snapped out of my drunken tantrum. Apparently, I'd been gesturing wildly with one of the bottles. I looked down and noticed the table was absolutely drenched in alcohol.

"Hey, let's get out of here. You need to learn to handle your liquor better, man. What's with you all of a sudden?"

"I said piss off!"

A dead silence descended over the entire restaurant. It was the sort of stillness that made your heart pound and sort of felt like waiting on the edge of your seat for the opening act to begin.

"Knock it off! Both of you!"

"How about paying and getting out of here?"

"Yeah, I'll get this. Just take him outside."

I could have paid for these stupid drinks too, you punks. I probably saved up more than both of you, just from part... part-time jobs! Is what I thought to myself, but all that came from my mouth was a few loud hiccups as Inyoung helped me stumble out the door.

"Get home safely, all right. Make sure Dongjoo gets home too."

I mumbled things under my breath to no one in particular and was reminded of that French thinker who said a man swears when he has nothing better to say. Yeah, silence probably was a better policy right now rather than cursing the entire world. I'd better stand here with my eyes shut and pretend like I have no idea what's going on.

"Look, sir. Please get him to Pangyo Station. It's just on the outskirts of Seoul. Hey, are you going to be alright? Call me when you get home, okay?"

I felt the cold through the window as I leaned my forehead against it, suddenly in the back of a taxi, apparently. Every time I was about to fall asleep again, the light from a street lamp flashed across my eyes. I suddenly remembered walking down the same street every day with my hands in my pockets, taking advantage of the sales events offered to high schoolers who finished their college entrance exams. That was ten years ago. I also thought back to the time I decided to take my future into my own hands by changing that fateful mistake I made. I was wearing a black down winter jacket. With my nose red from the cold, I put on the most serious expression I could muster, opened the door to my home, walked in, and sat down in front of my parents.

"Mom, I've made up my mind. I want to spend another year outside of school studying to try to retake the college entrance exam."

"You can't be serious?"

"I am. So, please send me to the best cram school that you can afford in Gangnam. My future is on the line. I won't stop until I make it into Sky University."

"Here you go again..." "Mom, please..."

My father sighed lamely, as though struck by the weight of some insurmountable and yet inexorable burden he must face. My mom chimed in.

"But, honey... Don't you think the universities you already got into are good enough? I mean, a few of them are in the top ten, aren't they?"

I felt my mother's own insecurity behind her kind, yet ultimately hollow suggestion.

"I couldn't stand to be seen going to those schools!"

"But all the other moms in the neighborhood are so jealous of how well you did, dear."

"I'm telling you; I could have gotten into Sky if I didn't mess up on question three. Please, Mom. I need this."

"But weren't there some questions that you guessed on and got right? I mean, what if you get a worse score this time around?"

Practical as always, my mom hit the nail right on its head. In fact, on the English portion of the exam, I completely blanked on question thirty and had to guess, which I was lucky to get right.

"No, I think I can really get in this time if I can just retake the test. Then, if I get good grades I'll end up going to medical school just like you always wanted..."

"..."

After this last, desperate plea we both had nothing to say and just stood there looking at each other incredulously.

"..."

Well, at least I shot my shot.

"Honey, sometimes it's also smart to stop and take a look around you once in a while after you've been working so hard for so long. You know, take a breather..."

This reignited the argument all over again, with me repeating my case to her several more times until I felt satisfied that I'd really dug the idea into her mind. Then I shut the door to my room and hid in bed. Work-life balance, huh? Someday I would bounce out of these sheets and get to work, alright.

All the alcohol I drank last night seemed to pierce my brain. Today was the last day of the computer programming employment program offered by the government. I knew my life was off on the wrong track ever since I had to choose the major I would study before applying to college. This locked my future into a single destination before I knew much of anything about myself. That morning, before leaving the house to go to my new programming-focused cram school, I walked out of the door with the image of my mother's wrinkled face blossoming into a wide grin.

I sat staring at the faces of the people I was studying with staring back at me through my monitor. We were all here to try to land a job in the IT sector and had been studying at this online cram school together for weeks. It was starting to become a close-knit group. I guess we could empathize with one another in here more than with anyone else on the outside. Everyone remained until the end of the program, without a single person dropping out of the course. It was almost like we'd been fighting the good fight together—side by side on the front lines of employment.

"You know, we never really had a moment to talk about it, but I think I've seen you somewhere before…"

"What? Where?"

"It's just, I remember the name Dongjoo Lee from this cram school I used to go to called the Elegant Math Academy."

"Wait a minute… you're *that* Jungmyung Park?"

"Hey, it *is* you! Dongjoo, I can't believe we're taking another course together."

I gave him a sheepish grin through the camera on my computer. "We met at one cram school years ago and here we are at an entirely different one. Nothing's changed but our age."

"I know, right? Hey, how did you make out in the end?" "I actually ended up graduating from Sky University."

"I always thought you'd make it. Me, on the other hand, I never got in thanks to this stupid mistake I made on question three of the math portion."

"Well, what else have you been up to since then? I double-majored in business administration before ending up here."

"Oh, a business major?"

"Well, my main subject was actually philosophy. Hey, I remember one time you told me you wanted to study existentialism. Ever get around to it?"

Jungmyung Park was an old ally from the trenches of cram school. So, he ended up getting into the best university even after being unable to hack it at Elegant Math Academy. I remembered how Jungmyung used to always debate with our ethics teacher about gender theory and Simone de Beauvoir's Second Sex. It really did make sense that he ended up pursuing philosophy in college.

"Yeah, but some good that did. Look at me, I'm right back to where we started. Even with a degree from Sky, it's not easy to land a good job these days. I had to do something, so I got into coding."

I was suddenly reminded of all the people at school who hid their majors like they had some sort of birth defect, especially those in the humanities departments studying things like literature or philosophy. Oh, Jungmyung, I used to think I could be different from everyone else, too. When I was younger, I was convinced I could go against the grain and succeed. Even you ended up retreating back into a business degree in the end...

"Hey, remember this, Dongjoo? That famous line about the handle of a fan from that novel The Square? How it gets narrower and narrower as you get closer to its base. Life's kind of like that fan, you know? You think you'll be able to do anything when you're older, but then reality hits and you end up just doing the same things everybody else does. I guess our fan is tapering out into this online programming school."

Like in Herman Hesse's *Demian,* tears began welling up in his eyes as he gazed off into the distance.

"You know, I had no idea who was enrolled in this class since it was all online. You were just a face in a little box on my screen this whole time."

"Weird huh? Anyway, you've got it this time."

"Hey, you too. I'll see you on the other side. Let's keep in touch."
Some people said that shadows exist only because of how bright the sun shines. Well, here I was, and I was certain that I would be the brightest sun in the entire interview room of M Corporation. I swore by the wrinkles spreading relentlessly across my two parents' faces

that I would make it this time...

"Hello. Please start by introducing yourself."

"Um, hello. My name is Dongjoo Lee. I'm applying for a position as a programmer. I have a strong foundation in coding and am sure that I've prepared harder than any of the other applicants..."

Dear Mr. Dongjoo Lee,

We are writing to inform you that based on your last interview, you have regretfully been dropped from the hiring process.

Thank you for your application, but we feel that you were not qualified for the stated position.

Even though we are unable to extend employment to you at this current time, we sincerely hope that you will continue to try your best in your future endeavors.

Never give up. With the effort and passion you have clearly demonstrated, we are sure you will be able to achieve your goals someday, whatever they may be.

Application number: 51012202

*

Back then, I was the same Dongjoo Lee who, after being turned down a total of two times, was eventually hired as a programmer at M Corporation. I suddenly hit my forehead against the taxi window. I look around and remember that I'm on the way back from the dinner near P Corporation that Youngbaek paid for. The alcohol almost comes back up as the taxi passes over a speed bump.

"Sorry back there."

I hear the taxi driver grunt this curt apology as we drift through the night, me in a state of semi-consciousness.

"Man…"

"Hey, it happens."

"Hey mister, do you know how much my annual salary is? I'm a software developer at M Corporation, all right? I failed the interview process two times and got my foot in the door on the third try! That means I'm no one to mess with, all right?"

"I see. Well, your parents must be very proud…"

The expression of the driver in the rearview mirror suggests he's just happy his last passenger of the night isn't any more drunk or belligerent than he already is.

"Yeah, but I… I didn't make it into Sky University… in the end. Ha!"

Red and orange tail lights bloom into patches of wildflowers outside the window. The throng of cars comes to a halt at a red light. A motorcyclist swerves through the gap between our car and the sidewalk, just barely making it through..

The Last Train

"Come on! Hurry up in there already!"

Echos bounce off the walls of the bathroom at M Corporation. Those still greedily occupying the coveted stalls hadn't come out for at least ten minutes. Everyone waiting starts to completely lose their tempers. I've got what feels like a ball of lead inside my stomach that I won't be able to hold much longer.

The anger is palpable. Everyone knows the stalls are occupied by fellow colleagues who are sitting there buying up as much stock in M Corporation's "M-start" as they can before the big public announcement. People always congregate in the bathroom like this to avoid detection, because we're not supposed to trade during working hours. Thinking to myself that if I don't make it in there soon, something terrible will happen, I suddenly feel a cold sweat run down my neck and back. The ceiling starts to turn yellow. The thought crosses my mind that instead of day trading, someone should be renting out toilet stalls to people who would pay a premium in times of desperate need.

By the time my vision starts to blur, the heavenly doors swing open and beckon to me as one of the stalls is vacated. At 09:05, five minutes after work has already officially started, everyone in the bathroom is either at the sink washing their worries away, or flushing their peace of mind down the toilet in the form of new, lucrative day trading opportunities. Two people talk about their holdings in front of the mirror.

"How much did you make?"

"Come on. With the size of my investments, I only ever make enough to buy the kids a pizza every once and a while."

In the tiny universe that fills the fifteen square feet of our company bathroom, we flush away all our troubles and concerns, especially those accumulated just outside at our desk terminals. Still, people say that miseries grow like hair, and as soon as you stop worrying about one thing you move on to the next. With my stomach finally relieved, I feel a new pang deep down in my guts thinking about how much money everyone else in here has been making since I first started waiting in line.

If you calculate the time it takes someone to day trade on the toilet for ten minutes each day and they earn an average of the cost of one pizza per trade, then if they did that for an hour every day, they would make something like a $300 hourly wage. While I'm out there, braving the confines of my office cubicle, they could potentially more in one day than my entire monthly salary.

As I leave the bathroom, I do the dance of pretending not to wipe my hands on my pants but doing it anyway. On the way back to my seat, I pass people sitting at desks with two large monitors on either side of them. The sound of their keyboards is like water flowing over river rocks. Passing by colleagues with headsets over their ears that line my path like streetlights, I get settled into my own chair.

"Hey, Dongjoo!"

The colleague sitting next to me pulls an earbud from his ear and casually looks over. He nods to grab my attention. I note that for some reason, he is here at the office instead of working remotely, which he usually does on Wednesdays.

"Why did you come into the office today?"

"Oh, I just have a few meetings. Anyway, did you get any?"

"What, M-start stock?"

"So, you do know about it."

"Think I'm going to sit by and watch everyone else get rich?"

"Well, have you heard of this guy? I made some decent money thanks to him."

He takes out his phone and props it up so I can look. "Who's channel is this?"

"I know you dabble in a little crypto, too, right? Have you heard of 'Val-You'?"

"Of course. He's famous. What's that he's always saying? 'You too have the value to escape poverty' or something like that?"

I look down at his phone.

"You don't want to slave away for the rest of your life, do you? This is your ticket to achieving your own personal financial freedom. In this day and age, you can rise up out of poverty simply by changing your mindset. Isn't something like that worth a try?"

"Hey, don't you think watching this is a bit risky, here in the office?"

My colleague answers by looking nonchalantly over both of his shoulders.

With similar feigned concern, I look to my left and right. Our colleagues all have their heads bent down and shoulders slumped in front of their monitors like withered trees leaning against a fence. The outlines of red and blue charts can be seen reflected on their glasses and foreheads. Only, they're not from their computer monitors but from their phones, eyes glowing in the light of their screens. Hey, if everyone else is doing it anyway... I mean, we're all in this together and in here with the same mindset. Just a bunch of caged animals doing whatever we can to escape from this zoo of a company.

"Well, if everyone else is trading right now, too..." My colleague nods his head in agreement.

"You know, at the end of the day, this corporation doesn't give a damn about us anyway. When we've run out of use, they'll clip us off like old fingernails.

Snip-snap.

"Wait a sec, I'm getting a message... someone's looking for me."

"All right. Hey, let's have lunch together later."

"Alright. Hey, let's have lunch together later."

I nearly went on living my entire life as an ignorant fool. Like a pearl shining silently to itself under several layers of mud. And I might have continued to live the sad life of a mere salaryman, until my meager existence was all but erased from this earth. Instead, I whip out my phone and take a quick look at the returns my cryptocurrency investments are making. It feels like checking for eggs in a chicken coop. My crypto is up 86%. I smile to myself and then look up at my monitor. I notice an email from the big boss himself.

Company-wide Announcement: Notice on a Certain Number of Executives' and Employees' Work Culture

Esteemed executives and employees,

First, I want to thank you for your continued efforts to pursue peak company performance despite the complicated economic situation we currently find ourselves in.

...

However, it has come to my attention that a certain number of you have given in to the recent market craze and began purchasing stocks and cryptocurrencies while on the clock. In particular, some executives and employees were reported to be seen in the bathrooms rather than at their desks past 9:00 a.m., which, we all know, is the start of our office hours. On behalf of the entire board of executives at M Corporation, I am writing to notify you that we are taking the current situation extremely seriously in the face of how this behavior can be seen to undermine our carefully-cultivated corporate culture.

M Corporation's top management, and I personally, will continue to stand firm against any internal or external circumstances that undermine our business environment. Please continue to do your best in seeing to your duties so that we are able to maintain our esteemed position in Korea and develop that reputation worldwide.

I actually laugh out loud. How is management going to try to keep the entire office from trading stocks and cryptocurrencies in the bathroom every morning when literally everyone does it? Still, I have to admit that I'm a little disappointed our CEO isn't the type of person to look the other way when us hard-working employees use a measly five minutes to make a little extra money on the side.

After the run-on sentence of the morning, lunch is like a much-needed comma in my day. After eating, I buy an iced americano. The cold seeps through the plastic cup and chills my fingers. My colleague from before leans over and makes this not-so-subtle brag:

"I actually have a consulting session with that streamer, "Val-You" later today."

"What?"

"Yeah, he gives one-on-one sessions on day trading and I figured I could use the extra help!"

He's so excited, I can almost see the caffeine seeping out of his eyes.

"So Val-You does consulting, huh? What do you talk about? How can I get in on that?"

"He helps you optimize your portfolio. He recommends stocks to buy, what's new in crypto, real estate... you name it. Cool, right? It's like rubbing shoulders with the true masters."

"And his advice actually helps your bottom line?"

"Based on what other people say, they're seeing returns of at least fourfold."

My own profits seemed like an old yellow candle in comparison to that sort of flash of brilliant, fluorescent light.

"Well, try it out and let me know how it goes. How much does a consulting session like that cost, anyway?"

"Sorry, that's confidential."

"Oh, come on. Well, at least tell me how to reach him."

At this point, he makes a dramatic pause and scans me up and down with his eyes like he's about to let me in on some truly secret information.

"Well, first of all you have to get an invitation to *Val-You*'s exclusive messaging group."

"And?"

"Look, I'll invite you. You need a recommendation from someone who's already in it. There's also a limit to the number of people, so you can't go around telling everyone."

My lucky day. Working for a top company, with solid colleagues like him, and I can see the path to permanent financial freedom just over the horizon... I bet one day I'll be an inspiration for others like me who had to work so hard to get where they are.

- You've been invited.

- Congratulations on receiving your invitation to your premium poverty solution, "Val-You Together!" where one of the top experts in the nation will help you achieve a minimum of 4 X returns via personalized consulting and real-time big-data-based analysis. Start down your path to financial freedom today using our premium poverty solution. It's so exclusive you need a personal recommendation from an existing premium member to get in!

You too can achieve up to 400% in returns using the free trading information we announce four times per day. When we tell you, press the "Buy now" button to buy, and the "Sell now" button to sell. Posting messages in the chatroom is strictly prohibited for all members except for "Val-You" and his management team. Any violations of this policy will result in your immediate expulsion from the group chat.

*Expulsion is permanent and non-negotiable.

Just like my acceptance letter to work at M Corporation, here was another lifeline that would lead me to financial salvation.

"Thanks for inviting me, man. I owe you one."

"Hey, what's the harm in getting rich together? Now, let's just try to make it through the rest of the afternoon."

Hunched over, the monitors on my desk stare back at me. My hand is sweating as I grip my phone in my pocket. The vibration I've been waiting for finally arrives. I pull it out and open the message in the group chat even before my phone stops vibrating.

- Recommended stock: PSDO
- Buy-in price: $5.03
- Projected increase: $5.57
- Selling price: $4.85
- Breakdown: $4.34
- *"Don't get too greedy with this one. Val-You and his team of analysts recommend you sell at the current price, take the 17% earnings and be satisfied. Anyone can make money working like a slave all day, but it takes a special kind of person to be able to create wealth without even lifting a finger. How long are you going to just sit there and twiddle your thumbs? Now is the time to start your personal journey toward greater wealth and guaranteed financial freedom with "Val-You."*

This has been your premium consultation notification for VVIPs with "Val-You Together"

I can't miss this opportunity. Not like how I missed the opportunity to go to Sky on account of that stupid mistake. But, for some reason, my brokering app doesn't load right away.

What is this, lag? Bad Wi-Fi? I wait for the message of what to do from "ValYou." Then, press, press, press! The messages from my company to attend the afternoon meeting aren't important right now. I'm sad I only have $1,500 left in my security account at the moment. This is it, the moment I make it big. I can already imagine the hundreds of thousands in crypto that will be coming my way.

- *"Buy now."*

Oh, no. I was a moment too late. But that's okay. My hands are sweaty. Red numbers broadcasting the recommended stock flash on my screen like my own heart that's about to burst with excitement. The number keeps climbing higher and higher. I can't miss it this time. When I try to press the buy button again, there's a pop-up that's asking me to enter my password. I curse out loud. I've already missed my chance at an easy $200 in the time that's elapsed. Another message from my colleagues pops up on my phone, but I'm too busy to even read what it says. Stop messaging me! It says I entered the wrong password for my account. Not again. I suddenly recall question number three on my college entrance exam. Calm down. Take a deep breath. I successfully enter my password. The buy-in price has already gone up from $5.04 to $5.25. So this is what fishing for a big catch feels like. Well, I can't miss this chance... . I buy-in at $5.25... Wait, what?

My hands are slippery with sweat. Sweat covers my forehead

and starts to drip down onto the screen of my phone. The $5.25 I bought in at falls back down to $5.14. I should have bought in the first time when I had the chance. I completely missed the delicious meal Val-You practically put on a platter in front of me. This can't be happening. Now it's $4.95. My $1,500 turned into $1,440 in the span of thirty seconds. Sixty dollars gone, just like that. That's two whole pizzas! I look for the sell button. There's no way I can lose four pizzas worth. I press "Sell." My account is at $1,440. Hardened like a fossil, I don't budge.

- *"Stand by. I'll check if there's another possibility for an increase."*

I missed *Val-You*'s timing again. I have no choice but to sit back and watch him orchestrate this battlefield. The stock price suddenly goes back up to the $5.25 I bought in at and I can feel a sick feeling scraping at my insides.

- *"All right, time to sell."*

- *"Hey, you impostor! How much do you get from this sort of manipulation, anyway!?"*

- *You have been blocked from the chatroom.*

- *"This stray that wandered in from the cold can't even recognize a steak when I put it right in front of his face. People like him deserve to live in the swamp of poverty for the rest of their sad lives. Permanently banned."*

I shove my phone back into my pocket. On my monitor, my angry co-workers are click-clacking away at me. Yes, yes... I apologize. My reply was late. I'm just a programmer that lost $60 in the last five minutes. At that rate, I would have been missing $720 from my paycheck for every hour that I stayed in there. I spin my chair around and head off in the direction of the bathroom.

"Hey Dongjoo, what's with you? You don't look so hot."

A senior colleague of mine hocks a thick, viscous loogie into the sink.

"I'm just a bit tired, that's all."

"Don't give me that. I can see right through you. Who was it? What did they do?"

"Aha... ha. No, it's nothing like that."

"All right. But keep at it. If you just work hard, you'll find a way! Got it?"

"Yes, I guess you're right... ."

"Just try looking on the bright side! Things are bound to take a turn for the better!"

Freedom

It's lunchtime at P Corporation. To get my caffeine fix, I step out of the cubicle area into the lounge where a group of coworkers stands waiting in front of the coffee machine.

"I am so, so sorry. I'll be out of your way in just a moment."

An employee with a lanyard ID like mine around his neck stands there watching with his hands clasped behind his back. A middle-aged woman in her fifties has her head bowed low as she hurries to refill the single-use paper cups next to the coffee machine.

"You should have refilled these before it became an issue. Now you're holding everyone up from getting back to work."

"I apologize for the inconvenience."

"If I'm penalized for taking too long getting coffee, are you going to take responsibility when my contract isn't extended? Well, are you?"

"Hey, that's enough."

There is complete silence. Everyone looks over at whoever stepped in on behalf of the woman. It's young Jungwoo, and this is the first time I've ever heard him speak in a firm tone like that. I'm startled by his vacant look and the long shadows cast under his eyes.

"Stop it already."

The cleaning custody puts her hands together and bows her head even lower, trying to appear as obsequious as possible.

"I'm so, so sorry. This is all my fault."

She looks at Jungwoo, who is staring straight ahead at the other employee.

"Where do you get off, picking on an old lady like this?"

I step in between Jungwoo and the other worker. The tension between them is palpable.

"Alright, alright Jungwoo. What's gotten into you?"

Jung-woo's eyes, which only a moment ago seemed to be on fire, suddenly lose their glow. He sighs deeply so that everyone can hear it.

"Please excuse me."

He storms out of the lounge and the only sound left in his wake is the glass door rattling as it closes behind him.

"All right, everyone. Let's wrap this up and get back to work. Time to start the day."

The other guy still stands there, head lowered but eyes looking up and surveying the situation. The disposable cups are refilled, the coffee machine is working again. Everyone goes about their business. I watch him pull out a cup, but he walks away silently without pressing the button to produce the espresso.

"Hey, Youngbaek! Happen to check SCR33N last night?"

It is the voice of Jiyoung Kim. She joined our team earlier than I did, so she was technically my senior, but we kept the relationship casual and friendly. I hear her clear, high voice penetrating the din of the people lined up to get their coffee, waking me from my morning malaise like the cry of a bluebird. Jiyoung was the same age, thirty-two, which made our relationship a whole lot easier. She greeted me with the same chipper smile every morning. It's actually one of the things I look forward to. Yet, today I'm surprised by her brazen and very vocal admission of using SCR33N. I mean, everyone does it but that doesn't mean you should announce it to the entire office while implicating me as well.

"Yeah, hey don't you think you said that a bit loud for this time in the morning?"

"Oh well, too late now. Anyway, did you hear the news?"

Of course, virtually everyone in the office had the app installed on their phones and checked it regularly throughout the day. We all tried to maintain some semblance of decency by pretending we were above indulging in all the gossip and trash-talk.

"No, what news?"

"That we, I mean P Corporation, is being broken up into several subsidiaries."

"Oh, that old rumor? Let me guess, you saw it posted on the company forum? It's been up there forever."

During my five years of working here, the same rumor about subdivisions had been circulating to the annoyance and fear of everyone in the office.

"Yeah, but this time it's actually happening!"

"Oh, just like last year? And the year before that?"

"I mean... it sounded real to me. Why don't you check for yourself? Hey, look who it is. Jungwoo! Looks like you woke up on the wrong side of the bed today..."

Jungwoo, who returned without anyone knowing, bows a quick greeting, and then comes over to talk with us.

"Ha... actually, I just needed to step out and wash my face for a moment. I guess I didn't get enough sleep last night."

"Huh, I pegged you for a morning person. Anyway, how you holding up newbie? Still like working here?"

"Oh, well... you know how it is. Ha..."

He laughs off Jiyoung's question. But I know Jungwoo isn't his regular amiable self right now.

"By the way, what was that scene all about, Jungwoo?"

He swallows hard and stares back blankly at me and Jiyoung.

"What happened? Did I miss something?"

"Look, I'd better get back to my desk before our team leader says something to us again. See you two later."

"What? Are you like hiding something? Haven't you learned that when someone starts getting on your case, all you have to do is tell them you'll work twice as hard? That's all there is to it. Anyway, you're right. Let's get back to work."

Sure, Jungwoo. Sometimes we all have our off days. I palm my coffee tumbler like the magazine of a gun and head back to my cubicle. All is quiet on my way through the office hallway as I make my way to my seat.

"Jiyoung! I need to speak with you."

Whenever our team leader has something important to say, he yells out across the office. Apparently he needed to see Jiyoung right now, and fast.

"Be right there, sir!"

"All hands on deck. I need managerial level and up to meet me in the big conference room immediately."

Suddenly, the office is bustling with employees folding their notebooks, straightening ties, and pushing in chairs.

"It must be true, then."

I can barely make out the managers' muffled conversation in the adjacent conference room.

"Hey, Youngbaek..."

I'm caught off guard by Jiyoung's uncharacteristically sullen tone.

"Yeah? What's happening in there?"

Then the sound of the Department Head's voice calls everyone into the meeting like the sudden proclamation of martial law.

"Sorry, I'd better get back in. Talk to you after."

"All right, but you'd better tell me everything."

The glass door to the conference room shuts with a sharp, cutting sound that sucks the air out of the office. Everyone left behind is dead quiet.

Only the lower-level employees remain sitting in their chairs. A long, muffled monologue can be heard through the wall of the conference room, which lies in the corner of the office. Following the speech, a murmur of protests can be heard rising like a steady drum beat. Normally, this situation would be a welcome vacation.

Having all the managers off of our backs for an afternoon was a rare event. Yet, for some reason, I find myself sweating in my seat. I try talking to sweet, innocent Jungwoo sitting next to me to ease some of the tension.

"Psst... Jungwoo."

"Yes?"

There was also something sullen about Jungwoo's tone today.

"Remember when you asked me if I enjoyed what I do?"

"Huh? Oh, sure."

"Well, all I have to say is that you should run while you still can."

Jungwoo's eyes quiver like small ripples across a cup of coffee.

"But... where else would I go? All I can do is try my best."

As expected, another overly earnest reply from Jungwoo, like some sort of automated answering machine. I smile and give him an encouraging nod. Oh Jungwoo, if only you knew that I am the one who truly has nowhere else to go...

"Hey, Jungwoo. Will you cover for me? I'm going to go get some fresh air."

"Certainly!"

I need to clear my head. I suddenly have the impulse to feel the wind on the twenty-eighth floor rooftop, which non-smokers rarely, if ever, visit. I walk through the silence of the office to the elevator that will take me to the top of the building.

Cold wind washes over the rooftop in waves while people puff their anxiety away into little white clouds of smoke. There is a mix of those either staring up at the sky, tapping their fingers over small tin ashtrays, or pulling sugary drinks from a row of vending machines. As though swimming against the current, I weave in between the groups and try to find an appropriate place to sit down.

One of the guys that joined the company at the same time as I did is standing there cradling his phone in his hands with a thin crease of concern visible on his brow. The heavy air of disquiet seems to stretch across the rooftop from one side to the other. I almost feel sad. It's like I'm watching the autumn leaves of my youth fading feebly before my eyes and falling into the stream of time.

SCR33N is in an uproar. The first volley of arrows is aimed at the HR department, demanding they take responsibility for what was looking like a massive wave of layoffs. There was also the fury of those who just entered the company and were now on uncertain footing. Seasoned employees were raging about having to take even more time away from their families to make up for the downsizing..

My head starts to throb just reading through the posts. Swiping down to refresh the feed each time reveals more of the same. I take my hand from my overheating phone and feel the coolness of the breeze against the pad of my thumb.

When I get back downstairs, a heavy expression lies on everyone's faces. The silence is stifling and hangs over the room like a damp rag. Jungwoo isn't sitting in his seat anymore. Something on his unattended monitor catches my eye. Oh Jungwoo, now this is the type of document that should never be left up on an abandoned screen for anyone to see, even if it's just me.

Jungwoo Lee_Resume for Position at M Corporation

Jungwoo, Jungwoo, Jungwoo... why did I have to be the one to catch you with this?

"Hey, Youngbaek."

Around this time, Jiyoung's usually announcing the lunch menu, twittering like a bird, but today she looks absolutely panicked.

The thing that makes me more worried than anything else I've heard today is the way she says my name like that.

"Jiyoung... what's happening?"

"Ever hear that expression of having a knife at your throat?"

"Sure, why?"

"Well, sometimes you hold the handle and direct it at yourself. No one makes you do it. At least, that's how I feel about this whole thing."

Of course, she meant to say that we were all personally responsible for staying with P Corporation for as long as we had. Posts about the subdivision were up there for ages. We really dug our own graves on this one. So, who is to blame here? The only way I saw out of it was to wake up and smell the coffee, face reality, and try whatever I could to get ahead. If only it was as easily done as said.

"... I'm sure it will all work out somehow. I don't know what was said in that meeting, but... I'm sure you'll be alright, right?"

"Ha... well, thanks anyway Youngbaek. That is so like you..."

On my way home from work, I watch the dull sunset out of the window in the back of the bus. Outside, the river flows beneath the bridge as though nothing has changed. Above the river, flowing through this day and on into tomorrow, over the weekends and occasional holidays, are countless smaller universes pushing the entire weight of their Sisyphean tasks before them.

As I sit and ponder what the leaves are thinking as they drift over the same water we drive across, I get the sudden urge to check SCR33N again. A few days back, a post was made about H Corporation by an employee who works there. It described some sort of illegal insider trading going on ahead of an IPO and was recommended to me by the algorithm as the hot topic of the day. The hundreds of comments attached to the post were like weeds tangled in the mud.

If You Feel it's Unfair, Then Find a New Job

Posted anonymously by H Corporation User 3456048

Why is it that our company is the only one being attacked for this sort of thing? Insider trading? Please. We all know that everyone does it in some form or another. In a few months, people will forget all about this little incident. It helps that it was all done using pseudonyms. So, who do they think is going to get caught? While you continue to blame your inferiority complex on the advent of the Internet, I'll be enjoying my retirement with a portfolio full of corporate stock options. It's not like anyone held a knife to your throat and forced you to work here. If it's unfair, work harder, rise to the top, and change things yourself. Otherwise, just shut up about it already...

└ *(Unlisted Workplace): A thorough investigation should be conducted. They shouldn't be allowed to get away with this while all the rest of us play by the rules!*

　└ *(H Corporation): People at companies too small to be listed here shouldn't chime in on things they know nothing about. Go back to grade school.*

└ *(H Corporation): Stop embarrassing yourself and your company. Have you no shame, sir?*

└ *(M Corporation): Don't all companies offer additional stock options, packages, or inside information as bonuses to employees?*

It's sort of funny to run into another person talking about knives at throats on the same day. I didn't know there was a company that paid out its bonuses in information, though. This is also the first time I heard that M Corporation, where Dongjoo works, also offers shares as compensation. I mull this over as I grab onto a bus handle with one hand and my phone with the other. Then, I shoot a text over to Dongjoo.

- *"Hey, quick question. Does your company give out shares as a bonus?"*
- *"Duh. Doesn't yours?"*

I stop and wonder why Dongjoo's messages are always so curt.
"Oh, well... actually we just get paid in additional salary."
"Look, you're smart. I'm telling you, you'll learn to code in no time. I'll even write you a recommendation letter. By the way, are you on your way home?"
"Yeah, I'm on the bus."
"Oh yeah? Well, guess who got to work from home today? LOL. I'm in my pajamas right now."

I suddenly remember something I heard in a video about how you might be in a toxic relationship and need to reconsider your friendship with someone if you feel like they're constantly mocking you.

"Right... well, don't work too hard."

I choose to mask my anger in sarcasm instead of engaging with

Dongjoo's blatant aggression.

Reading Youngbaek's petty message from the comfort of my own room, I feel like I've racked up some serious points for today. Even though Youngbaek went to a better school and his family had enough money to cover the down deposit on his house, it was thrilling to see my investment in our rivalry finally start to show some returns.

"All right everyone, that's it for today's meeting. Please do whatever you need to in preparation for next week's sprint and make sure to log all your remote working hours."

Finished with work for the day, I tear my headset off and fling it across my desk. My stiff back pops as I get up from my chair. I head over to the bathroom wearing a yellow-stained shirt. The door creaks loudly on its hinges as I open it.

"Is that you Dongjoo? Are you done with work?"

I'm so used to her yelling at me like this, without even looking I can see her feet padding across the floor as she leans out of the kitchen, her hands holding onto the door frame.

"Do you want me to make you something to eat?"

"I'll do it myself, mom."

I slam the bathroom door shut. The hinges are so old, it takes two or three times until the door fits in place, but it still leaves a small gap you can see in and out of next to the frame. I wash away the sweat and dead skin that's accumulated on my hands from sitting at the keyboard for so long. Whenever I tell her I can do something fine on my own, it's like another weight is added to my mom's crushing obsoleteness. I can picture her laying on the single-size bed in her own room, sighing and worrying about how to somehow make herself useful.

After taking off my shirt, I scrub it in the sink with soap to try to get some of the yellow out. The water falling down the drain reminds me of the incessant cooing of my mother. Good job today, son. After a quick rinse, the gray water washes down the drain along with the realization of how utterly poor we are compared to the rest of Seoul. The floor and drain that leads to the sewer below are concealed by a thin stream of water that connects right to my sink. I move to the edge of the bathroom where it's drier so the water on the floor doesn't seep through the holes in my plastic slippers and make my socks wet. Then I wring my wet shirt out and shake it so hard that its echo reverberates through the entire house.

I hear the murmur of a video playing on the other side of my mom's door.

"Here are five ways to communicate more effectively with your Gen Z son or daughter..." and then, "My son says he can't find anyone to marry him because he doesn't have enough money..." I dry off, pick up my phone, and notice that my hands feel silky-smooth after doing that bit of laundry.

- *"+ 120%"*

Checking my coin exchange app full of red lines and charts for the twentieth time today, I see the $100K I borrowed from the bank under the pretext of starting an honest, small business, is now sitting at $220k. Nope, no matter how many times I refresh my screen, the return rate continues to read +120%. Still, not bad.

I've already made more than someone would have made saving $20K a year for six consecutive years. If this goes on for just one more year, I'll be able to attain economic freedom in my early thirties. Gripping my phone like a microphone, I imagine myself in an interview years later on how to make it big. I croon at the reporter's questions about how I managed to become a member of the financial elite.

Yes, that's right. My name is Dongjoo Lee, and I guess I'm best known for being a self-made man. First, let me start by saying just how lucky I am to be here. But, you know what they say, fortune always favors those who wait. Living my entire life through the bars of cheap semi-basement one-room studio apartments is what helped me make up my mind to become rich... no matter the cost. I never stopped believing in myself every step of the way. I only made it by constantly assuring myself that I would one day be able to cast off the shackles of poverty and see my face boldly reflected in pure sunlight on the surface of a river. One day I simply made up my mind. It probably helped that I was always surrounded by the complaints of drunkards and petty people fighting over things as trivial as what college they went to.

I know somewhere deep inside that I am destined to fall asleep in a bed at the very top of a high-rise apartment listening to the gentle sound of the wind. These scars of poverty and academic exclusion will be covered up with crisp new bills until they are no longer recognizable.

The One Left Behind

It's Friday afternoon at P Corporation. The day's work seems to be on schedule with no major hiccups to deal with. Sunshine slants through the windows and falls to the floor of the office casting the cubicles in a golden light. I haven't seen this side of the office in what feels like a while.

"Hey, you are all free this evening, right?'"

A summons from our team leader for yet another company dinner. Everyone hastens to come up with a good enough excuse for not being able to attend. Some seem to have prepared ironclad excuses in advance. Others spit out quickly assembled sentences that sound like a large language model AI might have made up. I say I have to take care of a sick family member. Jiyoung has a previous appointment she can't get out of. Of course, Jungwoo, the newest employee, says he can attend without a moment's hesitation.

"Sorry, sir. I have another thing to go to tonight..."

"No, Jiyoung. No way you're getting out of this one. Without you, it will just be a bunch of dudes sitting around a table. Plus, the next team over is coming out too."

It's funny to hear the rest of us described as dudes in this testosterone-soaked company of ours. I've been working for five years, but I still can't understand why gender is so important for team morale when it comes to eating with your coworkers. Jiyoung just stands there and the atmosphere in the room feels like my five o'clock shadow. Of course, Jungwoo is quick to pipe in with another exemplary answer of his.

"Team leader, um perhaps Jiyoung is excusing herself so us guys can let loose without having to worry about having a woman around."

Classic Jungwoo, transparent to a fault as always.

"Well, what's this important thing you have to go to tonight, anyway? Is it a date or something? Come on, we haven't had a team dinner in ages. Think of the team here, Jiyoung."

"Ha. Well, if you insist on me answering that..."

I'm right beside her and can see the last message Jiyoung posted on her messaging app from where I'm standing. The last photo she sent was an image of what she ate for lunch. Apparently she had a $100 session with her personal trainer lined up tonight. The photo was followed by a string of crying emoticons. I guess she really didn't want to miss this session at the gym after the huge lunch she ate.

"Anyway, when Jiyoung gets married off we won't be able to see much of her, so we better enjoy her company while we have the chance, right boys?"

Jiyoung turns her head and bites her lips, letting out an inaudible sigh.

"Ha! That's the spirit. So, Jungwoo, where did you make the

reservation for?"

"I reserved a table at your favorite spot, of course. Is everyone ready to head out? "

We pack it in for the day. Jiyoung slings her purse over her shoulder roughly and the cosmetics inside make a sharp rattling sound. This clearly isn't how she planned to spend her entire Friday night…

We enter a barbecue restaurant and sit down. Jungwoo is busy playing bartender at the end of the table. As the youngest, he has to juggle refilling Soju glasses and beer mugs so that the more senior members surrounding him never have to face an empty cup. For his next trick, he pours a little bit of Soju into two overlapping shot glasses, then tosses the shots into mugs of beer, like christening them with holy water. This makes for the classic Korean company cocktail. One part resignation, two parts mindless joy. Our team leader, sitting opposite Jungwoo, looks across the table at everyone with a boyish smile.

"Let's drink as much as we can here and then call it a night. No pub crawl today. Everyone's thought of a good toast, right?"

At least he's merciful. He just doesn't know how to connect with people outside of drinking. I didn't have time to get an AI to make an acrostic out of my name for the toasts tonight. He makes us do this every time. Maybe I can come up with something that will serve as a shining example of my hard work ethic and the bright outlook of our company's future right here on the spot. I rack my brain to come up with what is probably my worst work all week, then recite it a few times in my head.

'Young'... *young!* And eager to please.

'Baek'... always at your *beck* and call! All day, all night!

'Kim'... will work for *Kim-chi*... that's right, I'm desperate here, folks!

Another Friday evening where everyone wanted to go home after work, but was now drunk enough to talk excitedly about themselves, laughing with each other across the table. I look up and see a framed landscape painting hanging over our table, staring down at us. I recognize it is a depiction of the famous Buddhist parable about a prince who dreamed he was in paradise only to wake up to reality. Yes, I wish this were a dream too. I hear our team leader talking loudly over everybody on the other side of the table but can't make out what he's saying.

"So, Youngbaek, what's new with you?"

Jiyoung, sitting beside me, prods me from my reverie.

"Well... I've actually been really thinking about getting into a certain something that everyone else seems to be doing these days... if you catch my drift."

"Oh, you're thinking about investing too, are you? So, that's why you've been working so hard?"

"Ha, well... So, are you into that kind of thing, too?"

"Ha! Of course, of course. Who isn't these days? They say you have to be an idiot not to invest, right? If you have any good leads on potential stocks, let me know first."

So, Jiyoung was into stocks too. If I don't get on this train now, I'll be completely left behind. Why didn't I start sooner?

"Everyone does it, right? And that's all anyone talks about on SCR33N..."

"I didn't take you for such an avid SCR33N user. Ha! Everyone in the app is always posting about the huge profits they're raking in. I wonder what I'm doing wrong..."

"Well... you have to start somewhere. Sorry, I'm getting a call. Who the heck is trying to reach me at this hour? Hello, Jiyoung Kim speaking..."

Her words trail off as I start to ponder how I can get my hands on some of those profits everyone else is making. She's right, I've got to start somewhere...

"Yes, yes. That's right. Anyway, how did you get my number again?"

Jiyoung suddenly hangs up and slams her phone on the table. I give her a sidelong look, inviting her to tell me what that was all about. When she doesn't tell me, I go ahead and ask.

"Well... who was it?"

"Oh, nothing. I get calls like this all the time from matchmaking startups trying to hook me up with some dude to marry. I treat it like spam."

"Oh... how come I never get calls like that?"

Jiyoung suddenly lets out a deep sigh.

"Say, Youngbaek..."

"What's up?"

"It's been a while since you got engaged, right? So, how's the wedding planning going?"

"I'm surprised you even knew we got engaged."

"I mean, your profile image is a photo of a big diamond ring..."

"Yeah, well... we're taking it slow."

"Look, we both turned thirty-two this year, right? So, I bet your parents are hounding you to get married. I know mine are. But working in Seoul... I mean, it's so hard for me and my boyfriend to find an affordable place in the city. Who knows when we'll be able to afford to get married."

What can I say? Even though I find myself in a similar situation, I can't seem to find any comforting words to tell her. I wonder if my girlfriend of ten years and now fiancé, Jungyoon, is worried about the same thing.

"I wish I could find a place in the suburbs. On SCR33N, everyone always talks about buying real estate as soon as possible. On one post I made, several people called me an idiot and said even worse things for not taking out a loan to buy a house sooner."

"Jiyoung..."

"Yeah?"

"I think I've heard this from somewhere. But you should just... try looking on the bright side. You know, things will take a turn for the better, right?"

"Ha. Ha... all right, Youngbaek. Thanks, anyway."

As soon as we stop talking, our team leader drunkenly drags Jungwoo with him over to our side of the table and sits down. My own vision starts to blur. Jungwoo's entire face looks beet red.

"Well, well... If it isn't Youngbaek and Jiyoung. At your age, I'm sure you're both busy trying to get married, aren't you? Just don't have your honeymoons at the same time, we're already short of people. Ha!"

"Have a lot to drink, sir?"

"You kidding? I'm just getting started. This is only the first stop of the pub crawl. Tonight's going to be a real knockout!"

"How about you, Jungwoo?" Feeling all right over there?"

Jungwoo answers me with his eyes closed tight.

"Yes. Thank you, sir."

"Hey, Youngbaek, did you know Jungwoo here is practically a master investor? He reads books on it all the time and was just telling me about it."

Jungwoo, who was about to gulp down a cup of much-needed water, puts it back down to respond.

"Ha. Ha... No, not really."

So, Jungwoo has already started investing in stocks. I'd better just listen. It's not like I'm going to share that I'm a resident of the infamous 85th floor with him or anyone else here.

"Well then, Jungwoo. What can you tell us about the market right now?"

"No, it's nothing like that. I just subscribe to a few video channels is all. I heard the creators of one of the channels I watch worked here."

"You mean Mr. Jung? He quit."

Jiyoung takes out her phone and pulls up his channel. *"Visit a doctor if you're sick, a pharmacist if you need medicine, and come to me, Val-You, when you're ready to be cured of your poverty."* One million subscribers. The sound of our team lead pushing his shot glass across the table to be refilled fills the silence.

"Hey, you all! Don't get any funny ideas. Everyone on this team is going to be rich someday. Alright?! Let's have another toast!"

All the shots people have been secretly tossing behind them or on the floor to avoid getting drunk is starting to pool around us. A few members from the team next to ours are hazing one of their new recruits. Then they start to lecture the poor guy about life. Trust us, nothing else is important. Money is all that matters. The recruit just keeps replying with the same answer— that he'll try to do his best, thanking them for their words of wisdom. I look around the table at who's left. All my superiors seem to have stepped away. This could be my only opportunity to escape. No one seems to be paying any attention to me. Jiyoung takes out a stick of lipstick, puts it on, then looks over at me knowingly. She smacks her lips a few times, then snatches up her purse. This is our chance. We head straight for the entrance. It's like you read in Greek mythology.

Look back even once, and you're stuck in hell forever.

I walk out of the door where the fresh air awaits us. Another successful escape. We make it to Gangnam Station in no time. A stream of people is sucked into the subway entrance. We walk down the station stairs together. In case anyone forgets, the words, *"It is illegal to film other people's bodies without their knowledge or consent"* are clearly posted on the walls. Seoul has always had a problem with perverts recording women in public spaces. We look over our shoulders and check to see if anyone else from our company has followed us. Jiyoung turns to me and says with a wry smile:

"Phew, we made it."

"That we did. Where do you live again, near Gunja Station?"

"Yeah, and you're headed in the same direction, right? This is our train, we better get on. It's going to be a while for the next one at this hour."

"Yeah, can you give me a second? I need to call my fiancé."

"Sure, I'll just make a similar call, I guess."

The subway emerges loudly from its underground tunnel and crosses the bridge over the river. Lights from the apartment complexes that span its banks spread a silver mosaic over the water. *Jungyoon... I finished my company dinner. Did you finish yours? It would have been nice to see these lights reflected on the water with you from a park bench instead of from here on a seat in the subway.*

"Youngbaek?"

"Yes, Jiyoung?"

"Things are bound to get better someday, right?"

"Of course."

"Look at those apartments over there. If you figure it costs about five million to live in each one of those compartments, that's five million per light shining on the river. There must be a whole lot of rich people in the world then, right?"

The lights from the apartments seem to float somewhere above the water without being swept up in its current.

"Ha... you're probably right."

"I work my butt off and can't even afford to buy one of those designer bags every girl seems to have."

Aside from the lights reflected on its surface, the pitch-black river turns the subway windows into mirrors. Jiyoung looks a bit drunk. I catch her glancing at me in the window. I try to maintain eye contact with someone else's black leather bag on the floor instead of locking eyes with her. I think I'd better find a way to talk about something innocuous, just in case.

"Anyway, what have you been watching? See anything interesting lately?"

"Look, Youngbaek... I'll just see you at work on Monday. I think I'm a little drunk... I'm going to make a personal call on the next car over. Get home safe, all right?"

"Yeah, you too."

Jiyoung gets up and walks over to the next train, swaying as she goes. I take out my earbuds. My fingers automatically find the video app on my phone.

Recommended Video: "Val-You - The Top Five Reasons Why Women in Their Mid-30s Can't Get Married"

This is an entirely new recommendation from the algorithm. When I skip to the next one, another video by Val-You automatically lines up in the queue. It's titled, "Korea's Fertility Rate and its Devastating Effects on the Economy" I know I'm being baited into watching it, but do it anyway. I skip to the very end to see his conclusions.

"The only way to save Korea and its economy is to have more babies and fast! The future of Korea will be left up to young parents like you. What's there to worry about!? If you enjoyed this video, don't forget to hit the like button and subscribe. This has been your personal poverty therapist, *Val-You*!"

I make my way to the video settings and press "Not interested in this video" instead. The subway heads deeper into Friday night. I find myself utterly tired and looking forward to sleeping through the rest of the weekend.

Next Recommendation: Book Review, 22 Ways to Overcome Your Fragile Mindset

*

My team leader's eyes are glued to his monitor. He hasn't budged since lunch started, but I know better than to do other work in the office. At least when the managers are around.

"Excuse me, but aren't you going out to lunch?"

"Oh, go on ahead without me."

Wait, what's that he's looking at on his screen? It seems even our team lead hasn't been able to avoid the current stock craze.

"Oh, um...Youngbaek. Do you... do you trade, too?"

Did I hear him right? Or is this some kind of mind game to get me to confess to using my work time for other pursuits?

"Uh, excuse me?"

"I asked if you did stocks too?"

Not at all, sir! As a former resident of the 85th-floor penthouse, I have decided to stop doing that sort of thing all together. If only he knew...

"No. Not really. "

"And what about you over there, Jungwoo?"

Jungwoo, who had been staring diligently at his monitor with a serious expression, suddenly looks up, surprised.

"Did you call me, sir?"

"Yeah, you. Didn't you hear what we're talking about?"

"Oh, well yes. I guess I play around with stocks every now and then. But, only in small amounts."

The team leader must have forgotten the drinking conversation.

Still, Jungwoo, Jungwoo, Jungwoo... that's not the answer you're supposed to give. If a new employee mentions they do stocks to their boss, of course, that's what they're going to think you do at work all day. I guess even you, who always seem to have the perfect answer to every question, slip up sometimes... Wait, maybe you're doing it right now just to show you're still human?

"Well, Jungwoo, have any plans for lunch today?" "Uh, no... no, I don't."

"Let's go down together, then. What sounds good?"

Suddenly, everybody on our team stares wide-eyed at our team leader who is asking our youngest member to eat with him. This never happens.

"Huh? Oh, I'll eat anything."

Lunch is in full swing. Everyone's waiting in front of the same old elevator that takes us down to the same old lobby that leads to the same old basement cafeteria with the same old lunch options. I look around to see if I can find Jungwoo. Twenty-eight-year-old Jungwoo is standing around as bland and awkward as the first day he came to this office. He has been looking a bit more haggard, though, if you looked closely. He's standing in between our team leader and the head of our entire department. I suddenly notice that all three of them are smiling and laughing together, like old pals. People flock to the elevator doors as the lights flash its arrival. When the doors open, it is already full of occupants from a floor below going up. Nope, not this one! The elevator slides back closed and the people left without a ride down cast imaginary rocks at the closing doors with their eyes.

"Wow, are they really getting on one of the elevators below and going up just so they can ride it back down before everyone else gets on? The nerve of some people!"

These words are merely more stones thrown by my colleagues that harmlessly tap against the doors. Tired of waiting for the elevator, many of us choose to skip lunch and take naps at our desks instead.

Sitting at my desk, the lights are turned off for the lunch hour. Several senior members of my team are already fast asleep despite the persistent sound of someone clipping their fingernails somewhere else in the office. It's far more tranquil now than when everyone is busy working. I close my eyes and lean back in my chair. I find myself staring at the SCR33N app before I even remember opening it. I skim through the same posts of people pretending to be living a new, special day each and every day, even though they look just as banal and unappealing as old cafeteria lunches to me. The clock reads 12:10, which means I have at least fifty minutes left until the lights turn back on. Concern weighs on me just as much as my drowsiness. If I do take a nap here in the office, what if I fart in my sleep without knowing it?

"Hey, what's everyone doing here in the office and not out at lunch?"

A light turns on like a sudden flash of lightning. The general outline of the office starts to become clear again. Certain parts of it are being illuminated as people come back from lunch early, even though our break isn't over. I look around to see where it was that the lightning struck. Our team leader is staring down the walkway.

"Is everyone in here day trading instead of going out to lunch, these days? Is that what good employees are supposed to do?"

I try not to make any rustling sounds as I quietly slip my phone back into my pocket without being detected.

"If you're going to be an office worker, at least try to act like one, all right? Aren't we paying you enough?"

It's been a while since I've heard the team leader get on anyone's case like that. I can see Jiyoung standing still with toothpaste still foaming at the sides of her mouth, toothbrush in hand. What if she swallows it? Jungwoo is standing a few steps behind the team leader, a cup of takeout iced americano in hand.

"I want everyone to check the email our CEO sent out today, alright?. Now, get back to work."

Then, just like that, our team leader's demeanor completely changes and he's back to normal again. The lights are on. Lunch is over. From across the office, I hear a surprised, yet subdued, "Oh!" as Jiyoung runs in the direction of the bathroom, sucking at the foam running down her chin.

The day fades into the afternoon. After lunchtime, I feel fresh, sharper even. Did that short nap somehow increase my IQ? My mind, which only an hour ago felt like my cluttered one-room apartment, is now neat and orderly like the data on a hard drive. Yes, hello! Assistant Manager Youngbaek Kim of P Corporation, at your service. If I manage to work everyday in this condition, I, Youngbaek Kim, could rise to the position of executive in no time. I almost want to type out how good I feel in a glorious email and send it out to the world. I know you must be busy, and thank you so much for your time, but please read my email and give me your re- ply by tomorrow. Thank you and sincerely yours, Youngbaek Kim! When everything's going as well as this, it feels like that same wonderful feeling you get when you hit enter at the end of an email. Whatever you've been working on, you finally get to send it out and be done with it. I wish everyone could see me in moments like this when I'm at my best. To stretch my stiff back, I put my hands on either side of the armrests and twist left and right. As I do this, I can't help but take the opportunity to look back behind me at the chair where our team leader sits.

Between the partitions of his cubicle, I notice he is looking intently at something on his monitor. I figure since I'm taking a break anyway, maybe now would be a good time to go to the restroom. I also kind of want to get to the bottom of his lunch date with Jungwoo. Almost forgot about that. Why did he ask me first whether I did stocks or not? Then he suddenly asked Jungwoo out to lunch with him. What did they talk about over their meal? What is it that he's so focused on? I get up and walk as naturally as I can in the direction of the restroom. On my way, I make a quick scan of what he's looking at while trying everything I can do to make it look like I am completely uninterested and respecting his privacy..

Shocking Housing Price Surge Precedes Controversial "Sales Permit System" Debut - What's Really Driving the Spike?

Seoul's Housing Prices Remain High: The New Neighborhoods Capturing Real Estate Agents' Attention!

PIR Index Hits 17.0: It Took Seventeen Years of No Spending to Afford a Home in Seoul!

If I stand here looking for too long, people will definitely get suspicious of what I'm doing, so I quickly shuffle off in the direction of the restroom. Crash! Bang! Rattle... now I'm sitting safely on the toilet seat in one of the claustrophobic stalls. I type in "How to start trading stocks" in my search engine.

Search Results: Start Trading Stocks at these Exclusive Prices

A mess of search results pop up like snares waiting to trap a novice trader like me. So, this is where all the online advertising money is being spent these days. I don't even know where to start. What useless search results. I almost forget to focus on the reason I'm searching in the first place. It's probably been just over two minutes since I locked the bathroom door. I check my social media. The pink balloons of posts from people I follow fill up my screen. These are people I will never meet in real life, But, where else will I hear the gossip on how everyone else is getting rich day trading in the bathrooms at work?

I get a sense of how much of a "big brother" state the online mediascape in Korea really is. As soon as I switch over from my search engine to social media, my social media feed is interrupted with things like "Apply for this Introductory Course on Stock Market Investment Taught by Real Experts." It's pretty disconcerting that my data was handed over and then regurgitated back to me in a matter of seconds. Trying not to think about this, I scan through what people are posting. I can't help but notice that Dongjoo is being as narcissistic as ever about his whole programmer persona thing. It also looks like Jiyoung went to a cafe during her lunchtime...

Coinchase – Your Cryptocurrency Exchange

Among the posts I thumb mindlessly through, I am suddenly sucked into this cryptocurrency exchange app. While up until now I've somehow always managed to avoid ads on social media, I guess today is the day when one finally gets me. Crypto wasn't that far from what I was originally searching for, so I feel less guilty when I download and open the app. I mean, advertising made me! I sign up for a membership. Now verify my account... One more layer of verification...

So, just like brokers in the real stock market tracing the red and blue figures across a big screen, this is where people buy and sell cryptocurrency. What a simple principle. Buy low, sell high. Float like a butterfly, sting like a bee! I too am a part of the hip new generation that is capable of making money both from a paid salary and from investments–all in the space of a few minutes in a tiny bathroom stall at work.

I start calculating every minute and second of my life that I'm not spending making money. The potential earnings I could be making unfold into a tapestry of charts and graphs before my very eyes. I figure I can make at least as much as my entire salary with a few well-calculated crypto trades. So this is how money is made! I've been an absolute fool this entire time. A fool that only knows how to put his head down and work hard for others. The people in all the videos I've been watching about trading, who have already achieved their own financial freedom many times over, seem to look back at me through my screen and laugh. They remind me every day that I am a fool for continuing to live the life of a simple salaryman. I come to realize that in the large scheme of things, my whole team, all my colleagues, and whatever hard work we do... is all for nothing.

"Just how long are you gonna be in there? People are waiting out here, you know."

Guess I lost track of time. I'm prepared to wait silently until someone else leaves a different stall before me. After waiting, when the time is right, I flush and walk out.

I shuffle back to my chair, my body sort of bent over as though the whole office was slanted at an angle. Since when was everything titled on this downward slope? I can still see those red and blue charts in my mind as I start drafting an email. Let's see, 10% of $50K is $500, so... If I can reduce my mealtime by a few minutes, I can spend that time trading crypto- currency and make four or five times as much.

My eyes sting and my spine feels twisted out of shape from wrestling with my phone in the tiny stall. The numeric charts in red and blue, when looked at from above, looked like a bowl of fruit salad that I could make little sense of. Still, considering I could be earning upwards of $500 in no time, it's probably worth it to try to learn more about it. By my calculations, $500 times thirty days is $15K, and that kind of money doesn't come free.

I sit down and turn on my computer. The switch feels heavier than usual. I guess my fingertips are already tired from the day's work.

Turning off my computer, the switch feels heavier than usual. I guess my fingertips are already tired from the day's work. I think about shuffling politely over to our team lead's desk to say goodbye. I turn my chair and see he is laying almost horizontally in his chair, staring at his monitor with a blank expression. Time to say goodbye. First, I take a look around to count how many people have already left before me. I slowly get up, pack my bag, and go over to bow politely.

"Wait a minute, Youngbaek"

Our team leader calls to me in a hoarse voice before I even get there.

"Yes?"

I know he wants to try to guilt trip me into staying later instead of leaving, but after he sees me noticing what's on his monitor, which clearly displays the fact that he's using this time to trade stocks, we both know his words have no power and I am off the hook.

"Never mind, get home safely."

Still, as I walk out, I can feel his stare burning through the back of my skull. I leave without even looking back. Jungwoo is waiting over by the elevator, leaning his head against the wall.

"Hey Jungwoo, haven't been able to escape yet, huh? Hey, is everything all right?"

"Yeah... I guess everyone upstairs gets off work earlier than us. I don't know how many elevators full of people have passed me by already."

I'm reminded again that everything, even riding the elevator, is all about timing—and people are ruthless. They will take an elevator headed up all the way to the top of the building just to get their spot on it before you on the way down.

"Haven't they fixed the elevator algorithm so people couldn't do that anymore? They said they would look into it..."

This tired tale about someone fixing the elevator someday barely registers with me. I've heard it at least a hundred times standing in this very spot.

"Ha. I hear you, man."

There's something in Jungwoo's tone, which is usually so bland and formal, that hints there might be something else going on with him. Four years his elder, I know that I'm expected to say something or at least ask him how he's doing to open up the conversation. Suddenly, the light flashes to announce the elevator's arrival.

"Shall we, then?"

Something about Jungwoo's voice definitely sounds strained. I nod attentively to everything he says. Did he just let a smile slip? It was subtle, but a smile nonetheless. Like a faint crescent moon. I barely make it into the elevator before the doors close.

Beyond the revolving doors, sunlight pours through the neat row of trees that lines the street. A few rays get caught up and concealed within the shadows as a cool breeze starts to blow. The frantic energy I've had penned up inside all day from all the coffee I drank leaves me.

"What do you usually do after work?"

Jungwoo is the one to pick up the conversation first.

"Oh, you know. Just relax. Watch stuff online. What about you, Jungwoo?"

"Well, I study a bit of this or that... or else I house-hunt."

"You what?"

"House-hunt. Like for real estate."

"Are you telling me you're already in the real estate market at your age?"

"It's never too early to start. I've built up a bit of pocket money and am almost ready to start looking into some real investment opportunities. It's nothing serious. I'm what you'd call a *propkid*[1]."

"*A property newbie, huh?*"

"Yeah, that's what they call us. Someone who's new to real estate."

I catch another glimpse of Jungwoo's discreet smile, only this time there is actually a little curl of real humor hanging at the edge of it. So, he could genuinely laugh about something after all.

"Right, right. Hey, Jungwoo, where did you say you live again?"

"Oh, I live in Gangnam."

As though each letter in the name carried its own weight, anyone who was lucky enough–no, rich enough–to live in the Gangnam neighborhood always recited each syllable with confidence. So, Jungwoo was from Gangnam, the modern utopia of Seoul.

"Wow, Jungwoo. Not too shabby."

Jungwoo, as though he has heard it before, and in fact, has heard it a hundred times, simply shrugs his shoulders and keeps walking.

"And where did you say you lived again?"

It's the first time in my life that an everyday question like where I lived feels like an attack.

"Well, it isn't quite Gangnam..."

Most people would die to be a resident of the greater Seoul metropolitan area, as the address on my ID card clearly displays. Yet, while the neighborhood I'm from used to be a soft brag that I would bring out when needed, now it feels like a mark of shame. You won this one, Jungwoo. What I really want to ask is whether he leases his place or rents it, but either way, well done. Any further questions would be gratuitous at this point. That's a checkmate, for sure. The wind between the buildings messes up my hair and I have to pause to fuss with it. Since I don't have anything good to say in response, I take out my phone and pretend to check it.

"All right, Jungwoo. You go on ahead. See you tomorrow, I guess."

"Yes, sir. Get back home safely, then."

It's six in the evening. I step outside and notice a building across the street that's casting its shadow over our office. I realize I'm not a raft gently floating down a stream at all, but a wad of toilet paper thrown off from the roof of the top floor. I still have so much left to do before the day is over. Post on social media, exercise, manage my stock portfolio, check my crypto, and, apparently, start learning about house-hunting on top of all that. What's next? On my way home, I assure myself there's nothing left for me to scour in the app, but my thumb instinctively finds its way to the SCR33N icon. As usual, the real estate forum is hot.

If you don't buy a home right now, you'll live to regret it.

What are you doing wasting your time and not jumping on the housing market? Economists unanimously tout the recent explosion in real estate speculation and investment as good for smart investors. Don't pay any attention to the naysayers who constantly prattle on about a future crash. They have no idea what they're saying! Any investor worth their salt knows that things like interest rates, supply, and demand don't apply in the same way to real estate.

Besides, what is slaving away at the office going to get you in the end? You're not the type to look at earnings from passive income like renting or subletting as something immoral, are you? If you haven't already, do whatever you can to become a homeowner now. Otherwise, when you look around at your friends later on in life, you will 100% regret not buying one sooner.

└ *(Unlisted Workplace) LOL, this guy's trying so hard.*

   └ *(Original Author) Looks like the homeless are already flocking to my post and leaving behind uneducated comments.*

└ *(P Corporation) Looks like the state of Korean corporations is causing everyone to panic and look elsewhere for their livelihood.*

   └ *(Original Author) There's nothing wrong with working at a company and getting rich on the side. Don't take your anger out on others, now :)*

└ *(M Corporation) Let's see your proof of purchase then. How can you post this dribble without even showing us your credentials? I bet all you've invested in is a homeless person's cardboard box outside Seoul Station.*

I see. The atmosphere in the comments section reaffirms my conviction that I'm way more of a prop-kid than Jungwoo when it comes to anything about investing in real estate. I guess no one but Jungwoo would ever admit they were a prop-kid. Still, I can tell just by reading the post that the author has no idea what they're talking about either. The comment section continues to fill up with fresh posts from people from rival corporations spending their evening talking trash about each other online.

It's Friday. I turn my back to the setting sun and stand facing the door to my empty apartment. A yellow sticker attached to my door lock lets me know that my gas meter is due for an inspection. I enter my four digits to unlock the door. The numbers of my password are rubbed off from wear, so anybody that cares could probably figure it out just by looking. I am welcomed by utter darkness. My head is especially full of competing thoughts and I feel more tired than usual. I toss my phone and then myself onto the bed, without even turning on the lights. It's so dark in here I can't tell the difference between shutting my eyes and keeping them open. In my mind's eye, red and blue charts race across the room, rising and falling in the darkness.

Above this image, I see the image of my fiancé, Jungyoon, waving at me out of the darkness. If I can manage to climb up just five or six of the blue and black charts, I think I'll be able to make it to her. Though she stands there calling out to me, the last few steps to get to her seem the hardest. Thank you for being my only semblance of support over the past ten years. If I can just manage to make it over this final graph, I promise I'll do whatever it takes to return the favor and support you for the rest of your life.

There must be a drunken fight happening somewhere outside of my window. Neon lights flash into the darkness. Glass breaks. The cops will be here soon.

- *"You asleep?"*

Now there's a coincidence. A message from Jungyoon waits for me in the corner of my bed shining from the crumpled sheets.

- *"Hey, I was just dreaming of you."*
- *"Really? What happened?*

I can't tell her that she appeared to me sitting atop a mountain of numeric charts of stocks and crypto…

- *"I dreamt I was falling. And you caught me."*
- *"Caught you? Ha! What do you mean? If I wasn't here beside you, that you'd fall to your death?"*
- *"Yeah, that's why you can never leave me."*
- *"If that's how you interpret it…"*
- *"Are you still with that friend of yours? How are you feeling?"*

It feels like my whole body is submerged in water. And still, I'm thirsty. I rub my blurry eyes because I was staring too intently at my phone up close right after waking up. I am just so, so thirsty. I pull open the door of my fridge with my toes, which is only an inch from where I lay in bed. All that's left is an unnamed plastic bottle with what appears to be a few sips of water.

- *"I feel fine. Maybe I'll come over when I'm done? Don't wait up."*

Is it just me, or are her messages getting shorter? I go over to the sink and fill my mouth with cold water. I get an empty feeling deep within the pit of my stomach. Like a hamster without a wheel, I pace around my apartment..

The Rubik's Cube

While everyone else my age goes out for a night of binge drinking, I sit alone at home on my bed scrolling through my phone. I check the price of leasing an apartment in Gangnam alongside the river. The cheapest one is going for four million. Youngbaek was really hung up about me saying I lived there. Bemusedly, I open the SCR33N app. A particularly juicy post catches my attention and I laugh a little to myself.

Is my man marriage-material?

Posted anonymously by a Doctor 281748

My friends and family keep bugging me about this, so I'm looking for some unbiased opinions. Do you think we are meant to be?

I'm looking for your honest opinion. Do you think we are meant to be?

Me:
Female, thirty-two
A Doctor
Owner of an apartment in Seoul, no debt
Annual salary $150K
Good family
No siblings
Graduated from the top university

Him:
Male, thirty-two
An average office worker
Rents, $80K in savings
Annual salary $65K
Easy-going
Eldest son of two siblings
Bachelor's degree from a decent university in the city

"Just look at this... does this girl actually think she's going to make the biggest decision of her life based on the majority vote from a bunch of strangers on SCR33N?"

A torrent of advertisements showers everyone every day with offers and advice for finding true love or a lifelong partner. Among the countless pieces to the puzzle of love, this person writes like she's only looking for a very few number of specific answers. Sorry, my friend, but love is more like a Rubik's cube than something that can be solved so simply. Like thumbing through a stack of bills, I scroll to the bottom of the post and see that it still has no replies. That's zero votes in favor of you marrying this poor guy.

What if I were in his shoes? Even if I don't have to take out my business card and place it on the table, everyone in this app can see that I'm from P Corporation by the tagline next to my name. Surely that's at least something to be proud of. Everyone else parades around SCR33N like high-born aristocrats, but do all of them really have the credentials to back it up? I'll show them what a real man looks like today. I'll tell the world I'm here and looking for real connection. I'll post whatever it takes... sitting here from my bed.

"Hello, I'm twenty-eight years old and looking for true love. Let me start by introducing myself..."

I'm looking to date someone out in the real world, but it can't hurt to post my plea here, can it? :) I live in one of the best neighborhoods in Seoul. You know the one. At five foot five, I weigh 147 pounds with 17% body fat. My parents are happily retired and would warmly welcome a woman into my life. I am calm and a bit on the quiet side but am definitely passionate. Once we get to know each other, I'm sure I'll open up to you. I believe in being rational but have a sweet side too.

I'm also constantly looking for ways to improve myself, and am especially confident in working in fintech. Sometimes I come off as a bit strong or forceful, but I'm really considerate of others. I spend most of my time at home, but I also like to travel. People say I'm handsome, but who cares about that?

I'm just looking for someone with similar tastes and values rather than external features. I'll take a hard pass on anyone that likes to go out and drink all the time or puts their friends over their significant other. If you're interested, shoot me a reply.

Thanks for reading this post and I hope to meet that special someone soon.

After writing it all out like this, I feel a bit embarrassed. Even some cosmetics ads don't go into this much detail about the products they're trying so desperately to sell. Before posting it, I check it one more time to see if I left in any identifying clues that might alert any of my coworkers. No name, no hobbies that would reveal who I am. Yep, I don't think there's any information that people would be able to recognize me by. I post it. Next, all I have to do is sit back and wait for my message to reach the community. This is what an eligible bachelor is supposed to look like!

Even though it's only been up for a moment, I swipe to refresh the feed a few times.

Zero likes, zero comments.

I swipe my thumb a few moments later, assuming there would be at least some sort of reaction by now. Anyway, if I do something else for a few hours, by the time I get back there will definitely be a few hits.

I go out of SCR33N and check my social media. One by one, my friends from school are all getting married. There are pictures of them at their weddings or all dressed up in photo studios with ceilings so high you can't even see the top. Photos like postcards fill up my screen—newlyweds leaving lavish Seoul apartments for their honeymoons or couples taking trips to the Maldives.

Mixed in with the idyllic posts of the friends I follow are a few celebrity wedding photos. I see news that a popular star actually married an average office worker like me. They posted a picture of their two children and dogs sitting serenely by a stream in the forest. For a moment, I catch myself thinking that that's how high you have to climb to find love these days. You either make it or are just a data point on a graph about the aging population and declining birth rate. You can't pitch a tent for your family to stay in if your monthly rent is a bramble of thorns. No matter how hard you cut them back, those branches just keep growing back to rip holes in your tent. Anyway, I don't want the family I start to have to live like nomads–or in tents at all, for that matter. I'll wait as long as it takes to get on the right financial footing first.

Enough time has passed. I should check SCR33N to see how many comments were left. I open up the app, expecting at least a few promising leads by now.

- *(P Corporation): Buddy, take my advice. No one wants to date someone that's five -foot-five. Give it up, dude.*
- *I mean, what would your friends think seeing you with a chick that's taller than you?*
- *(Unlisted Workplace): Yeah, just quit while you're ahead.*
- *(Certified Doctor): Hey, you don't sound so different from me and I made it out fine... don't listen to these other guys.*
- *(P Corporation): LOL. Yeah, but that's only because you're not a simple office worker like the original poster. You actually have a real job you can rely on.*

Seeing the tagline, "Certified Doctor" next to the only positive post makes even me laugh at my own situation. Oh, so this doctor that is the same height as I am, who probably went to a better school and makes more money than I do was able to find true love. It reminds me that despite how much I make each month, the interest I have to pay off on my loans makes me a less desirable mate out in the real world. Getting into one of the top companies and having its title next to my username doesn't mean anything at the end of the day. I thought I would be royalty amongst the SCR33N users, but it's just not the case. There are always more stairs to climb. Stairs upon stairs upon stairs... . I guess Korea's ancient class system of endless hierarchies, has really only changed in name. It will continue to loom over my life and the lives of future generations to come. Still, climbing endless stairs is different from the impossibility of climbing up a family tree. Instead of engaging the nice doctor, I decide to take my frustration out on the person that posted from P Corporation, who I think should have taken my side.

"Hey, I see you frequenting this forum and bet you're no taller than I am. We both work at the same place, too. Jealous much?"

"You talk big for such a short guy."

With that, he launches his counterattack in the comments section. I'm not going to lose this fight.

"I bet you're already in your thirties, aren't you?"

"What's it matter to you if I'm in my thirties or not?"

"What kind of guy would want to date an old lady like you? You're past your prime. Give it up already."

"Still, no one in their right mind would ever think about dating someone that's only five-foot-five. No woman is ever going to want you, trust me."

"You're trying too hard, old timer."

"Whatever, I'm done talking with you. Consider yourself blocked."

My opponent disappears forever from my SCR33N account, but our conversation remains. Through this exchange, I catch a glimpse of what I might become when I turn thirty. I wonder what kind of person I'll be after spending a few more years fighting with myself and others just like me in comments sections like this.

I do feel lonely, though. Outside of my parents, who won't be around forever, I try to imagine the family that I might one day have. I bet there's someone out there going through the exact same thing as I am. I sit and try to figure out why my lot in life has been like this and start to feel bad for my mom. My father too, for that matter. I guess this is just the best I can do. Maybe someday I'll meet someone who will be able to rid me of this feeling. There's nothing wrong with wanting that. No, everyone does deep down inside. No way I'm going to let those comments get to me. There's just no way.

Your original post has been removed by one of our moderators.

Even though I know that I'll never meet these people and they have no idea who I really am, still, the hair on the back of my neck stands on end. The taste of this defeat is bitter. Even in an anonymous community like SCR33N where you can run and hide at the first sign of conflict, this sort of thing happens. It feels like a slimy palm just slapped me in the face. The sweat from my hands and pressure from my thumbs start to cause rainbow-colored marks on the screen of my phone.

It's the same whether I'm at work or in the privacy of my own home. I can't seem to catch a break anywhere. I have a moment of pure pity for how pathetic my life truly is. It's added to the constant weight of being responsible for starting my own family someday. I think of all the other men out there holding up their spindly umbrellas against this torrent of desperation with no real end in sight. I swipe back to my home screen and see the time is 10:30. An hour and a half left before I usually fall asleep. If only I hadn't already spent so much time writing that self-introduction, I would probably watch a few videos before calling it quits. I get a notification that says Val-You just uploaded a new video.

I must have been frowning without realizing it. When I take my eyes off my phone, I feel the deep furrow that's formed between my eyebrows relax a bit. At this point, I should probably just wash up and call it a night.

The water is cold. It still needs time to warm up as I awkwardly wait outside of the stream of the showerhead, careful that it doesn't hit me. Water pours out in a torrent as I wait for that perfect temperature. I imagine the pathetic self-advertisement I posted earlier, and all the comments being washed down the drain. All the relationships I've built over the years also wash away. All I'm left with is a row of mismatched tiles on this Rubik's cube I've been trying to solve, reflected back at me in the bathroom mirror. Will I ever find someone who is willing to marry someone like me?

*

I'm sitting next to my friend on her sofa. Even with her five-year-old beside us, it's turning out to be a quiet Friday night.

"Jungyoon, what do you think of that guy?" "Which guy?"

She points to some man on the TV.

"Look, he must be shorter than like… five foot five or something. If he didn't have the job he has he wouldn't even be allowed on 'Couple Match' in the first place."

"Couple' what?"

Barely listening to what my friend has to say because I'm busy looking down at my phone, I pretend to follow whatever she's talking about the TV we're watching.

"Are you telling me you haven't heard of 'Couple Match' yet? It's super popular."

"'Couple Match?' Sounds kind of lame."

"I can't believe you haven't heard of it. You need to take more time off work or something."

"What, so it's like another one of those boring dating shows, out of literally hundreds?"

"Whatever, this one is way more fun."

She launches into this whole explanation about how they actually cast real-life, ordinary people, so it makes it so much more realistic. One participant was ugly but was a really good talker. Another was kind of on the tall side but took really good care of the way he looked. Why are these simple traits all these shows ever care about? It's always just a caricatured cut-out of someone's personality...

"I mean, just look. Don't you think she's way too good for him?"

"Huh? How should I know?"

"Come on. You can practically tell how much he's worth just by looking at him."

My phone vibrates and I look down at it.

"Let me just finish up with something first, then I promise I'll pay attention."

"Whatever."

There's a new message from Youngbaek. His name is saved with a cute little nickname on my phone that I recognize immediately.

- *"Are you still with that friend of yours? How are you feeling?"*

My friend takes her eyes off the TV for an instant and catches me texting.

"Who are you talking to anyway? I bet it's Youngbaek..."

"So what?"

On TV, the second male candidate is struggling to hold a conversation with the third female candidate. My friend lets out a sigh of disapproval, but I'm not sure if it's about the characters on TV or my own life decisions.

"Anyway Jungyoon, about Youngbaek..."

"Yeah?"

"Do you really think he's on the same level as you?"

"What do you even mean by that?"

"Well, for one, you're a licensed professional and he's only an office lackey... don't you think you should meet someone more in your league?"

"Are you serious? What are you even talking about?"

"I'm just saying... you'd be doing yourself a disservice if you didn't meet someone that earns at least as much as you do. Get real."

This old friend of mine, who usually brings a bit of needed sunshine to my life, is saying things that would test anyone's patience. She knows I've been with Youngbaek since we were both in our twenties. That's practically forever. Only four years ago we would have been satisfied sharing a cup of ramen between the two of us in a tiny one-room studio apartment. Just yesterday, it was so sweet when he said that as long as we stay together, we can get through anything. I mean, I think he even had tears in his eyes when he said it.

"It's not like you two are really going to get married or anything."

"How can you sit here and say these things when you know how long we've been together?"

"What? What I'm saying isn't wrong."

"I can't believe you're sitting here and telling me to break up with my boyfriend. You think you know everything since you popped out a kid?"

"……"

"But honestly, Jungyoon. Level with me here. I'm saying this as your close friend. Don't you think Youngbaek's just isn't a good enough match for you? I mean, at the end of the day, he's just a salaryman and always will be. Shoot, if I made as much as you, I'd probably put off marriage altogether and ride around in a Porsche all day."

This was coming from the same person that used a picture of her and her husband and child as her profile picture. Just the other day, she posted about how they were able to buy an apartment in the middle of Seoul for her mother-in-law. Why was she acting like she didn't care about family all of a sudden?

"Jungyoon. Listen to me. Marriage is a whole other issue."

"Like I don't know that?"

"Then listen to me! You need to find a marriageable man. One that suits you better. Oh, my poor baby! Don't cry! Mommy's here…"

I look around me at a bag of premium, Grade-A organic health snacks on the table, sitting in this 1,200 square foot apartment with three rooms, a 65-inch TV, and framed wedding photos scattered throughout—pictures with big, bright smiles on them.

"Come on, Jungyoon. Think about it. If you stick with him any longer, people are going to start thinking that you're selling yourself short... There are so many other great options out there... I know you and Youngbaek are high school sweethearts, but that can only get you so far... Plus, that's like all you have in common. I mean, really! Oh, wait a minute. I just got a call, it's my mother-in-law. Yes. Uh-huh. Oh, you're coming over now? When will you arrive?"

Am I starting to doubt myself? What if I am making the wrong choice with Youngbaek as everyone seems to be telling me? Am I being too naive? Immature, even? I look back at Youngbaek's message, which I know he probably sent after a long, tiring day at work. I bet he sent it right after he got on the bus, before closing his eyes, his heavy lids fighting against the gentle sway of the public transport.

"Look, I'd better go. It's getting late, anyway."

"No, no! Oh, why did I open my big mouth? Now I regret saying anything at all. Anyway, it's all completely up to you. It's your life, right? Try not to think too much about it. And don't get me wrong, because I only said all that stuff because I care about you."

On my way home, I tell Youngbaek a harmless lie—that I had a good time at my friend's place. When he asks how I'm feeling, I also don't have it in me to tell him that my stomach actually does hurt. I wonder when my friend got it into her head that I'm such a premium, Grade-A person... What I really want to do is talk it over with Youngbaek and get it off my chest, but I know he probably had another tough day, so...

All right, so that is how other people view our relationship. And sure, marriage is a whole other issue. I know that getting married in Korea requires photo shoots, multiple dresses, makeup, an expensive venue, honeymoon planning... It sets the average couple back what, $100K at least? So, people are happier marrying people in their economic league. That's what everyone says, at least. Marriage is a union of families, not just individuals. Does Youngbaek expect to be able to support both of our parents in their old age with his salary? If it was just about how much money we made and had saved up, that would be easy. No, we have to plan for their retirement too. First, they'll want to know how much we have allotted for the wedding. Then we'll have to take them out to a nice hotel, do the bridal shower, and all that. This is an important stage of life, right? We've got to put our best foot forward, no expenses barred. Otherwise, what will everyone think of us? At the very least, the man has to buy a place to live with whatever money is left over, otherwise, how would he ever be able to show his face in public?

I log into SCR33N. The algorithm is showing me that happiness is an apartment in Seoul with two children and a Porsche in the garage. I quickly write up a post and decide to leave this debate about my future happiness up to a majority vote. I check the comment section to see the results.

Is my man marriage-material?

Posted anonymously by a Doctor 281748

My friends and family keep bugging me about this, so I'm looking for some unbiased opinions. Do you think we are meant to be?

Me:
Female, thirty-two
A licensed specialist
Owner of an apartment in Seoul, no debt
Annual salary $150K
Good family
No siblings
Bachelor's degree from the top university in the nation

Him:
Male, thirty-two
Your average office worker
Rents, $80K in savings
Annual salary $65K
Easy-going
Eldest son of two siblings
Bachelor's degree from a decent university in the city

I'm still unsure whether I've summarized all the main points that should go into my decision about what might end up being the most important choice of my life. Should I just take it down? I leave it up for the community to weigh in on... out of curiosity. Staring down at what might very well be a mistake, the screen of my phone suddenly changes. It's my mom calling. It doesn't stop ringing, so I answer. As I pick up, I get this weird feeling of vertigo like she was looking at the same screen I was just staring at a moment ago.

"What are you up to, dear?"

"Oh, hey mom. I'm on my way back from seeing a friend."

"Who? That nice married girl who bought her parents a new apartment?"

"That's the one."

"So, what did you two talk about? Did you have dinner together?"

"You know... this and that. We watched this new matchmaking show that just came out."

I sit and listen to her go on and on about this cousin of mine who still can't find a job. Then she tells me about one of her friend's sons that keeps failing his college entrance exam and retaking it. Just when I begin to wonder what my actual mom has been up to instead of these random other people, she suddenly pauses, inhaling sharply.

"You know, Jungyoon. As your mother, I have to tell you I do not like you seeing that Youngbaek boy. We worked so hard to get you where you are. I don't want you to squander away your life."

"Mom, how many times have we been over this? You're not the

one that's getting married!"

"Still, I'm the one responsible for marrying you off. If I don't tell you these things, who will?"

"But mom, it's my life..."

I find it hard to end that sentence and my words sort of trail off.

"I gave birth to you and think my opinion deserves some respect."

"Here we go again..."

Any opinion of mine loses all power against those words. If she expected this much of me, maybe she shouldn't have had me in the first place. I start to feel sick again. In her mind, happiness only comes with owning an apartment in the middle of Seoul with two kids and a life like everyone else.

"Listen to me. I'm your mother. Call that nice doctor I told you about. The one that graduated from Sky University."

"Mom, I'm going to hang up the phone now..."

Of course I know what's best for me. Still... when everyone around you keeps telling you the same thing over and over, maybe you're supposed to at least entertain some of what they're saying. Try to see it from their side. They're just trying to help me, right? Maybe this is what's been giving me so much anxiety lately. By now, the post I made should have at least a few votes in favor of or against us being together. I sit down, open SCR33N, gulp, then swipe my thumb to refresh the feed and watch as the comments pour in.

"What, are you insane?"

"Get out of there while you can. You're way out of his league."

"What, is someone holding a knife at your throat and making you date this guy, or something?"

"He must be gas-lighting her."

"You know your parents are going to cry tears of blood if you actually go through with this, right?"

"Yet another innocent couple is torn apart by the SCR33N community. LOL."

Is it that easy to find a man who will promise to do whatever it takes to make sure his family lives comfortably? A man who will promise over and over again to take parental leave himself, so you don't have to give up on your career? How would these people judge him if they knew that he once carried me piggyback all the way to the emergency room one morning at dawn? What would they think if they knew he never once forgot to write me a love letter, or how when we first met he was working at that mediocre manufacturing company, starting from the very bottom and making his way up?

1. Appearance
2. Occupation
3. Personality
4. Financial Assets
5. Parents' Jobs
6. Academic background

Like examining the different sides of a Rubik's cube, I measure the two of us up–side by side–to see which parts will fit. I guess I am a bit out of his league if you look at it. Everyone but me is whispering in my ear how much better off I am than him. The majority of my post's voters on SCR33N are practically staging a sit-in on the app because they rate me so much higher. I can't get to sleep, so I reach for my phone.

- *"Youngbaek, can we meet up next weekend?"*

With the first cool winds of autumn starting to blow, bringing an end to the draining humidity of the summer monsoon, Jungyoon sits on a park bench by herself in front of a lake. I walk over to her.

"Looks like you beat me here!"

She sits there staring up at me, her face pallid and colorless. I suddenly realize I left home without a warm enough jacket. The cold breeze cuts me to the bone.

"Wait, what's... what's wrong?"

Ages seem to fill the space between us, whisperings of all the years we've spent together. I recognize in that moment already half of what she brought me here to say has already been said, without a single word spoken. She says it with her eyes. My hands clam up. I know she already knows what I'm going to say. No, at this moment I have no idea at all what to say. Please, just don't say anything.

Withered leaves scuttle across the pavement, breaking the silence with their nervous scratching across the ground. A few get caught in the wind, circle around, and come to rest at Jungyoon's feet.

"You know you can tell me anything."

"Youngbaek..."

"Yes?"

"This... is the end. I'm here to give you back the ring you gave me. You can try to sell it, but you probably won't get all your money back..."

She says what she came here to say and just stares up at me blankly, immutable as a diamond.

"But, Jungyoon…"

It feels like my brain is about to run out of my nose and drip down onto the pavement.

"I closed my savings account to come up with the money to buy a house with you… I even joined the company your parents wanted me to so we can be together."

"Youngbaek, I want you to try to be as realistic as possible right now… I mean, do you really think that you and I could ever have gotten married together? We just aren't in the same league."

I'm shocked by this sudden outburst of what must have been some sort of pent-up animosity. Why? Where did it come from? How long had she felt this way? I had no idea it would happen like this. I guess on some level it does make sense. I mean, who was I kidding? What kind of future could I have ever expected to have with Jungyoon? Not with the money I was making. The best thing I could have done to prove my love for her was to let her go so she could live the life she deserved with someone else. I guess I sort of saw it all along but pretended not to understand. All these years, I couldn't admit it to myself or her out of fear of actually losing her. Well, too late now.

"You don't mean it, do you?"

"Come on, Youngbaek. I mean, marriage is a whole other issue. It's the real deal. In what world could someone like you and someone like me ever really be together?"

"……"

I said that I would die for her, that I would do anything in the world for her. Still, there's nothing I can do to change who I am or the parents I was born with. The same parents that raised me with their own sweat and tears. I guess the past ten years we've spent together were all just a fantasy that I made myself believe.

"Wait, did you make this decision on your own?"

A pause in the conversation. A moment of silence that establishes the new sense of distance that has irrevocably formed between us.

"Yes, I made this decision on my own. This is what I want. Look, I'll transfer you the money and if you don't have anything else to say, let's just leave it at that."

Jungyoon gets up and walks out of my life. Just like that, ten long years evaporate in the space of ten minutes. Tears stream down my cheeks and fall to the floor, pebbles falling into a puddle. My vision blurs. Right, it is because of me. Because I was born the way I am, something I'll never be able to change, no matter how hard I try. I numbly check some notification that pops up on my phone. It lets me know that Jungyoon has blocked me. Just like that. I feel myself lifted up over the glittering water of the lake and washed away into a dreary delirium.

Only four years earlier, I was just starting out as a new employee at P Corporation. Sipping iced americanos at an intersection in Gangnam, still oblivious to the trials of office life and what it would have in store for me. An idealistic youth, offering a diamond ring to the girl I loved, in full belief that I had found the one. This illusion turned out to be an errant thread that was easier to sever completely rather than to untangle.

All I can do is wish her the best. At least I am still standing, though the dreams of my youth lie crushed underfoot. Looking back at my life, I see a trail of dreams drifting down a stream never to return. Then the river ends and I am left in absolute darkness.

My eyes sting. I take out my phone, then skim through my contacts for someone to talk to. I go through the entire list three times. Dongjoo's name is the only one that stands out. I press the call button.

"Dongjoo..."

"Hey, what's up? Why are you calling me at this hour?" "Listen, Dongjoo. I'm... I'm sorry."

"Whoa, what are you talking about? What's with you? Is everything alright?"

"Well..."

"Whatever happened between us, don't worry about it. Wait, where are you right now?"

"No, it's nothing like that... I um..."

"What is it then? Are you at home right now? Look, if it's serious I'll come right over. You're going to be okay, right?"

It's cold out. May azalea petals, touched by purest snow, be placed at Jungyoon's feet. I only ask that she tread lightly across the trampled flowers of my heart until the day she meets a more suitable man than me. Sitting on the same bench where she just was, I let time slip away and the night envelops me. Then, from somewhere out of the darkness, I hear the sound of feet running from far off.

"Youngbaek! Hey, Youngbaek!"

It's Dongjoo. He really came.

"Shit, I thought you were going to jump off a bridge or something. I took a taxi all the way here from across town. What's the matter?"

"We finally broke up."

"What? With your fiancé? You're kidding, right?"

My body convulses into sobs.

"How could someone like me ever get to marry a person like her? I had to let her go..."

"Ha..."

I'm unable to voice the futility of it all. I can't believe I even thought we could get married without even being able to provide a proper house for her to live in. Winter is coming and I can't get the image out of my mind of pink azaleas falling to the snow. Freezing on contact, they turn a bright, resplendent crimson.

Hanging from the Cliff

When I come to my senses, we're sitting at a table at what looks like a fried chicken restaurant. Dongjoo must have taken me here. He says I should eat something, even though eating is the furthest thing from my mind. So, Dongjoo is really the only friend I have when it comes down to it. He starts talking.

"Look, you should at least try to eat a little. Don't worry, this one's on me. Think of it as payback for all the times you took me out."

"Sure, thanks."

"I feel for you, man. So, you guys broke up today, or what?"

"Yes."

"Whoa, man. Something get caught in your throat? You're tearing up again. Here, wash it down..."

"I can't eat this. Let's just drink or something."

The number of empty bottles on our table starts to pile up. One more bottle, please! Yes, one more bottle for us two over here. If I could, I'd drown myself in this stuff.

"So... tell me. Why did you break up?" "I have no clue what I did wrong!"

Why is everyone in the place looking at me all of a sudden? Are we being loud or something? Whatever, go ahead and stare. Look at how poor and pitiful I am for being born low and being forced to give up on love.

"Youngbaek!"

Dongjoo clenches his teeth and stares across the table at me with a stern expression.

"Sorry. I'm fine. No, really... sorry everyone."

I'll just let it all hang out. Right here, right now. I don't want to go home tonight and see my sad story posted on SCR33N for the whole world to jeer at. No one will have to join a special hearing just to listen to my bad luck.

I think of Jungyoon's mother. Sorry, I didn't live up to your expectations. So, so sorry. Sorry that I was born with a plain old wooden spoon instead of a silver one in my mouth. And to my own mother and father, who raised me as best they could. I'm sorry that this is all you're going to get for all the effort you put in. Sorry! While I'm at it, I'm also sorry for blaming it all on you, who couldn't have done it any other way even if you wanted to. I know it's not your fault. Our little family, all huddled together eating with our wooden spoons... that's just how it was.

"Hey, Youngbaek. Are you falling asleep again? Are you even listening?"

"..."

"Here, have some water. You know what, how about a Coke instead?"

"Mmmm..."

Ding dong! Way over on the other side of the restaurant, someone stands in the doorway wearing a helmet and a mask covering his face. *Ding dong! Order for delivery!* The delivery guy stuffs his phone back in his pocket and heads back through the door laden with plastic bags full of chicken. Wait, wasn't there something about that delivery guy that looked familiar? Or is my mind playing tricks on me?

He looked exactly like Jungwoo. I could have sworn it was him. The youngest member of our team, our little Jungwoo Lee. Just imagine, the real estate expert himself, standing there in a doorway with a helmet and mask delivering chicken. I must be delirious.

"Hey, Jungwoo...!"

But some distant part of my brain tells me otherwise, that it can't be him and I'm just a sad drunkard in a chicken restaurant. Jungwoo owns real estate and lives in a rich neighborhood far away from this shabby little place in a no-name part of town. The automatic bell sounds again as Jungwoo, the corporate suck-up– wait, I mean this random delivery guy–walks out.

"Look, Dongjoo. I need to go to the bathroom. Okay?"

"Why? Need to throw up?"

"Just gonna... wash my face."

I'm starting to see the whole world clearly. This thing with Jungyoon has really opened my eyes to how the world really works.

"Should I be worried? I'll check on you in five. Go on, then."

"I mean, a breakup is a breakup, right? Screw it! I'll be right back."

"Yeah, sure man. Just come back, all right?"

I stand in line for the men's restroom. Was that guy Jungwoo or not? It's killing me.

A shiver runs up my spine and I let out a sigh of fleeting pleasure. Then I zip up and turn to wash my hands in the sink. Two eyes stare back at me in the mirror. They seem to belong to a youngish-looking man of thirty-something years.

The eyes are the eyes of the Youngbaek who went to Sky University. A Youngbaek full of pride with having landed a job at P Corporation. They are also the eyes of Dongjoo, applying again and again for the same job, proud of eventually becoming a successful programmer all on his own. They also belong to Jungwoo, with his delicate crescent smile just barely visible. The image fades and I'm staring back into the eyes of a desperate and drunken man. I kick a paper towel on the floor toward the dirty bathroom door.

I rub cold water on my face and neck, then tear two paper towels from the dispenser and dry myself off.

"Phew..."

"Jeez, you scared me. When did you sit back down?"

Dongjoo takes his eyes off his phone for an instant and looks up at me. Then he returns to the video he was watching.

"Let's head out as soon as this video is over. It's almost done."

"What is it?"

"Ah... just some guy. His channel is called "Poverty Therapy" or something like that. Ever hear of him?"

Of course I did. That was Mr. Jung, who left P Corporation not so long ago to pursue his fancy new poverty-free life. His face was always glowing these days. What was his secret?

"You know... I used to work with that guy."

"Really? You mean he used to work at P Corporation?"

"Yeah, he even gave everyone a bottle of wine as a gift when he quit. Anyway, what about him?"

"Didn't you know he has this private group you can join? I'm a VIP member. He gives me tips on day trading and stuff."

"Huh."

We both look down at his phone. "Visit a doctor if you're sick, a pharmacist if you need medicine, and come to me, *Val-You*, when you're ready to be cured of your poverty."

"So, what kind of tips does Mr. Jung... I mean, *Val-You*, give?"

"Check it out. This is one of the private VIP videos he sent."

"Listen to me when I tell you that it is truly shameful to be poor in such a highly-developed country like ours. Our parents and grandparents didn't claw themselves out of the Korean War to leave us without a dime to our names, did they? You don't need to sit idly by and let the people with only the best degrees take all the wealth for themselves. Anyone can do it. So, why are you poor, then? The truth about poverty is that it's all just a state of mind. In today's era, where making money is incredibly simple, that excuse doesn't cut it anymore. Do you know how hard it was when I was growing up? Now I count myself as one of the lucky ones. For I have seen the light at the end of the tunnel. People, trust me, poverty is a dirty disease that can now be cured."

"Watching this guy's videos has really made me rethink a lot of things. He's completely changed my view of the world."

"... really?"

My eyes open wide and I reel in my chair. I have a moment of realization. I think back on all the countless hours I spent staying up all night, trying to decipher cryptic charts and graphs on my own. It may not be a sin to be born into this world poor, but it is most certainly a sin to leave it so. Does that mean I've been living as a sinner, gradually advancing toward a thankless death? I stare up at the ceiling. Has my entire life been like a piece of sushi going round and around on a conveyor belt?

"You know, Youngbaek, you can join the VIP membership too if you're interested. They're always looking to recruit new members, but you have to be invited by someone who is already in."

"Hey, Dongjoo."

"Yeah?"

"You're thirty-two years old, right?"

"Yeah, we both are. And?"

"How much do you think someone our age should have saved up by now?"

"..."

A chicken leg chewed down to the bone sits silently on the table between us.

"What kind of question is that? Why are you asking me this sort of stuff all of a sudden?"

"Well, you asked why Jungyoon and I broke up... so?" "Well, I've probably saved up about half a mil in total by now."

"Really? You have that much saved up?"

"No, not in savings. That's just how much I've made. I'm around $100K in debt..."

Bits of chicken skin and crispy crumbs catch my eye across the table. Now Dongjoo's turn to ask me.

"How much have you managed to save?"

"Hold up, Dongjoo. How much do you think you would say you have if you were posting it on SCR33N?"

"What do you mean? I asked you the exact same question. What's that have to do with SCR33N?"

"Because every person on the app always claims to be a millionaire and own their own house."

"You're wasted, man. Of course, everyone's going to lie about what they make to people online"

"Exactly."

"So, how much do you have saved up?"

I wipe some of the crumbs off my shirt. My ears feel slightly sensitive to the people getting drunk and yelling at one another across the other tables.

"Look, Dongjoo..."

"Come on, I told you. Let's hear it already."

"I guess... I've saved around $100K, then."

"Let's have a drink."

I pour the rest of the bottle into a glass until it reaches the brim. I was too impatient. Instead of beer, the empty glass is filled with an undrinkable foam.

"To us..."

I gulp it down. Whenever our glasses are even partially empty, I quickly and sloppily fill them up again. No, we can't have any empty glasses at this table. My glass is filled again and again with foam, masking its actual emptiness. *Hey, careful! What's with all the foam, man?* Ah, it's good to be drinking. Is there any better way to conceal your vanity than drinking beer with a buddy? I fill another glass to the brim with pure foam.

One, two, three... I try to count the number of empty beer bottles on my fingers but keep forgetting the tally and starting over again. My empty cup, which only a moment ago I could have sworn was full of foam, now reveals its glass bottom.

"Hey! What if I had been born with a silver spoon?"

"I know, right? You and me both..."

"At least you graduated from Sky"

"At least you became a programmer!"

"... do you know how hard I've tried all this time to get a leg up on you?"

I am so sorry, Dongjoo. For everything. But, at the end of the day, I'm just an empty glass, so anything you saw or got from me was probably just a bunch of foam. Isn't it the same with you? Still, you were the only friend that came to mind when I really needed someone. For that and so much more, I'm sorry.

"All right, Dongjoo. You win..."

"All right, so tell me why you really broke up then."

"Nice try."

"All right, all right... cheers, then!"

I remember I have to work tomorrow. Yet another day where I'll have to do everything I can to avoid the drinking and chain smoking after-hours parties that my bosses are always trying to get me to go to.

"Let's go."

My stomach hurts. I look up. My head stretches across the sky like the crest of a Roman helmet. Or something like that. All I wanted to do was live a good life, just like everybody else. I went to all those cram schools, passed the entrance exam, went to a good college, paid my tuition fees and my dues. I even landed a safe job... Heck, the job I had was better than average. It was all right, in fact. Thinking about the injustice of it all, my mind goes blank. I curl up in the waves of my drunkenness and let them overtake me. The only thing I'm sure of is that I'll have one hell of a hangover to reckon with when this is all over.

Ding dong! I stumble across the threshold of a convenience store. *Welcome!* How is it that every single convenience store employee says hello with the exact same tone and pitch? They must be trained on an automated machine or something. I buy something to help my impending hangover.

"That will be $5, please."

I hear the muffled sound of a "Thank you!" coming from the phone of this convenience store employee.

"What... what are you watching there?"

I suddenly realize I'm asking something totally off the script that this poor employee would have learned in his training.

"Excuse me?"

Something about his expression makes me instinctively put up my guard too.

"Oh, I... I asked what you were watching. On your phone."

I realize that I'm behaving like a creep right now. I try to look at the situation from outside of myself. Yes, definitely creepy, maybe even a little threatening. This poor convenience store employee.

"Wait... I'm sorry. Forget about it."

"No, that's okay. It's just some mukbang channel that everyone's watching."

The employee sits back down and continues to stare at his phone like I'm not even standing in front of him. I can make out some of what's being said in the video.

"If you enjoyed this video, don't forget to hit the like button and subscribe! A big shoutout to everyone that donated to my channel or joined my Supportreon. For all you dreamers out there that fantasize about quitting your jobs and doing what I do, guess what? It's harder than it looks! Stick to your day job and leave mukbang to the professionals. Do you really think you could eat ten bowls of black bean noodles every day? Give me a break!"

A grin forms on the bowed head in front of me.

Twist and pop! The slightly carbonated hangover remedy I bought, a sort of fermented tea used in traditional medicine, hits the back of my throat in that old familiar way. All I need now is to be back in my own home. I mean... back in the home that I'm renting. That empty feeling I had earlier starts to dissipate like the strong odor of fried chicken that is slowly fading from my clothes and my hair. My eyes still burn, though.

"Do you really think that you and I are in the same league?"

The goddess of my dreams, who once beckoned at me over a towering mountain of red and blue charts, ran away in search of greener pastures. The least she could have done was break it to me softly, instead of trampling over my heart and our ten years together. Anyway, good luck finding someone that's six foot tall and a lawyer or doctor or whatever. I bet you'll find someone who grew up with a silver spoon in his mouth just like you.

I suddenly miss my dad. Those tired, sweaty parents of mine who raised me as best as they could. Mom, please call tonight to ask whether I'm doing okay. I broke up with Jungyoon earlier. Apparently, we broke up because of my worthless job and hopeless future. Because I'm not capable of doing what it takes to make a decent living, like filming myself eating ten bowls of noodles and posting it online. I should've paid closer attention to the stock exchange. Or become a video creator. I could have started some sort of online shopping mall as a side hustle, or gone to an even better university... . I should have applied for a better company, instead of trying to just take it step by step... I studied hard, went to work every day... and that's part of the reason why we broke up. I needed to be more. I needed to prove my worth by making it big, getting rich doing day trading, hitting the jackpot, or something. But, I didn't...

A sparrow flying by a granary can do little to prevent himself from heading in to steal a bite to eat. Even if I pity myself like this, what could I have done differently? I open my phone and search for a video to distract me, even if only for a moment. The list of algorithm recommendations includes this brutal one: *"Five Reasons Office Workers Are Doomed to Spend Their Lives Alone"*

Look, I was born into this life. It couldn't have played out any other way. I can do little to change my past now. My whole body rebels against the hopelessness of my reality. Still, I can't help myself from pressing the button to watch.

"The fact is most people don't understand even when you lay it out for them. All you have to do is pay attention and think smart. It's all about when to hold and when to sell. Still, nobody listens.

Isn't that right, *Val-You?*"

"Yes, it's sad, really. But, nothing comes easy. My patients—that's what I call them, by the way—are mostly afraid that they'll be poor for the rest of their lives. They get to the point where they feel so deeply impoverished that they believe that they'll never find a way out. Then, to make themselves feel better, they go online and criticize other people who got rich while they couldn't. People who earned their wealth by making an honest living."

"Exactly... And that's precisely why we've published this new book for our VIP subscribers. Trust me when I say that this single book has all the answers you need."

"Let me tell you, it wasn't easy to fit everything into one book. But, we somehow did it! And at this price, it's a bargain. We're practically giving it away!"

The video switches to a close-up of *Val-You* demurely holding up his new book to the camera.

Crash Course Credentials; You Too, Have the Val-You to Make it Big!

It feels like all the strength in my arm, which already seems to be clinging onto the edge of some sort of immense, indescribable cliff, is starting to fade. I don't think I can take it anymore. No one, including myself, has the right to humiliate me and push me to the brink like this. If this is how the world really works, then I, Youngbaek Kim, at thirty-two years of age, a fifth-year assistant manager of P Corporation, the second-largest company by market cap, just want to slowly back away from this cliff's edge.

Crash! A safe landing onto the sofa in my one-room apartment. My head is spinning and I feel nauseous from all the alcohol. I run to the bathroom. The pain of throwing up in my chest and the back of my throat combines with hot tears that gush from my eyes. Surprisingly, when I look down there's a splash of blood mixed in with all the rest. A sour taste comes up from the very pit of my stomach and there's a metallic aftertaste in my mouth. As I rinse, I discover a nasty cut across the lining of my cheek. How did that get there?

My eyes begin to adjust to the darkness of my room as I sit there. My phone, barely visible and off to one corner, is blinking and buzzing. I think to myself that there lies the true source of all my pain. That little device that can let me see how everyone else is living and access the torrent of lies and false hopes online. Still, I reach out for it and mindlessly swipe through to the SCR33N app. The thought passes my mind that I need some sort of physical cage on my phone to prevent me from checking it.

*

I jolt awake. There are still dry tear streaks lining my cheeks. My eyes are red and swollen. It can't see farther than a few feet in front of me. As expected, my everyday life was lying in wait, ready to spring at me. It's 9:32 a.m. Work started at eight. I'm screwed. I search frantically for my phone.

"Shit."

I was way over my limit last night. I finally find my phone. Ten missed calls. Today is starting off to be a total disaster. The icon in the corner tells me that my battery is only at five percent. I must have forgotten to connect it and set an alarm. I start looking for my portable battery to charge it on the bus, but can't remember where I put it. No, there's just no time to look. I'll make something up to explain it to my team leader on the way. Wait, didn't he ask me to finish that thing and have it ready on his desk by this morning? Just try not to think about that for now!

I don't even have time to check to see whether the door locks properly behind me or not. The electronic sound it makes grates against my ears. It seems like the starting gun to a frantic race. As soon as I'm outside the safety of my apartment, every second feels like part of a countdown. A cold sweat runs down my back, completely overpowering the warmth of the sunshine on my wrinkled shirt. I'm short of breath, hangover raging. I spot the bus I need to take pulling up to the station I am supposed to be at. It shuts its doors and creeps slowly away without me.

"Just a moment!"

But today's driver has no sympathy. I try everything I can to get the driver's attention. To get him to stop for me.

"Ha..."

At this point there's little difference between being thirty minutes or an hour more late. The result will be the same. I think this to myself as I sprint down the street. After a while, I give up on trying to hail a cab at this hour, then catch my breath and take a look around me. A basket of strawberries radiates brightly, all bunched together outside one of the stalls of the open-air market. Everything in the late-morning air looks so clear and crisp that I can't help but let out a sigh of appreciation, something I find funny to be doing in my current state. There it is, the next bus. Let me just call my team lead and let him know I'm on the way... Oh, my battery! Only four percent left.

A ray of sunlight brushes the skin on the back of my neck, warming me for a second. I feel sensitive to everything. Of course, this day was waiting for me after everything I had already been through. My failed sortie into the stock market, having to cancel my savings account, getting dumped by the woman I love... I'm so far gone at this point, I'm not sure that anyone in the world can help me get back. My head is reeling and my heart is broken. At least my bus is here. I can see it headed for this stop from down the street. Even as I wipe my tears with one hand, I pat myself on the shoulder with the other, encouraging myself. Come on, don't you want to go to work?

I scan my card and climb into the bus. As usual, the card reader greets me with its loud and overly-cheerful greeting, as though begging me not to look so sad.

Beep!

I scan my card and climb into the bus. As usual, the card reader greets me with its loud and overly-cheerful greeting, as though begging me not to look so sad. I see one available seat in the back of the bus. I let out a sigh of utter relief, thankful at least for being able to sit down and ride in some semblance of comfort. In the corner of my phone, I note that only one percent remains. I catch myself instinctively logging into my social media account. My phone shuts off. The colorful pixel display goes dark and all that remains is a gray reflection of my face reflected on its empty screen. The face I sit there staring into is neither smiling nor frowning. It just is.

I look out of one of the broad, sunlit windows. A flock of pigeons is busy pecking at pieces of bread under a telephone pole. They turn their heads this way and that, pretending not to be interested, and then peck away again. These pigeons remind me of a time I held a bag of chips in my hand and a group of four or six looked up at me inquisitively until I crushed them up in my palm and threw them to the birds. Pigeons everywhere are indistinguishable, just like these ones pecking at the bread outside the bus window.

I can also see myself, dimly reflected in the window. A young man bent over a rectangular piece of glass and circuits. I stare down at the phone in my palm trying to decipher why I'm always sitting here, on the bus, frowning over this little piece of technology. *What are you even doing? The Youngbaek reflected in the glass exasperatedly asks. Did you get what you wanted? From all those social media posts? Or, did you sit there and cry, drying your tears while you choked down those bitter-sweet bits of digital connection?* This line of thinking starts making me feel sad again, so I look away from my reflection and stuff my dead phone back into my pocket.

On this late-morning bus ride, the sun spreads throughout the bus, enveloping everything in an amber hue the color of sesame oil. I start to notice the other riders. Pairs of adults sitting together or other people my age with earbuds in their ears. It's been a while since I simply sat on the bus and looked around me. With my phone locked, the world opens up. Beyond the bus, the buildings seem to reach up to the bottoms of the clouds. Electronic displays that span entire buildings feature angelic sirens dancing enticingly, their advertisements whispering to me.

Have you ever seen a ring quite like this one? If you give a ring like this to your lover, she will promise you eternity. I guess that means all those lovers who can't afford rings like those will have to skip out on eternity... But never mind that... Maybe things will look up, afterall? I'll finally stop living a life chewing on stale cereal hoping for a kid's prize. Perhaps this little detour is just one of many valleys in the undulating graph I have to traverse to eventually marry Jungyoon someday....

The beautiful women in the ads pass out of sight as the bus turns a corner. Like those pigeons pecking at bread, everyone on the bus has their eyes on their laps, busily tapping away at their screens. I take a sweeping look around. Not a single person isn't staring down at the portable mirror in their palm. Pigeons picking out the marshmallows from children's cereal. Glued to social media and video channels they watch with the mindless hope that one day they'll discover the one true prize promised to them across literally every platform. I barely make out that my stop is the next one as the speakers of the bus advertise the same old thing they always do:

"Do you want to work far away or close to Seoul? All your friends are doing it. This could be your ticket to success!"

Stepping down from the bus with feet that feel like soggy pieces of bread, I'm already exhausted. The revolving doors of my building feel especially heavy today. The fourteenth floor... fifteenth floor... the elevator goes much faster when everybody is busy at work and I'm the only one riding it. Maybe today won't be so bad.

"Have you lost your mind?! Think you can just show up whenever you want without calling?"

"I'm... sorry, sir."

"Well, get to work, then. I'll deal with you later."

I don't have time to think about anything else. The first thing I do is secure a charger for my phone. I have to resuscitate it, stat. Charging, my phone emits a welcoming green light. I press and hold down the side to start the engine. The screen doesn't respond immediately to my touch when I press it because a thin layer of sweat–and maybe chicken grease?–is left over from the last twelve hours.

"Youngbaek, why are you so late, you little devil? Oh wait, I can smell the alcohol on you from here. Ha!"

Jiyoung squawks at me across the office like a raucous peacock.

"Please, not right now. I'll tell you everything... later."

Jiyoung's expression tells me she's already looking forward to buying me an iced coffee and hearing all about it. She sits back down and excitedly swivels her chair to face her monitor.

My mind is absolutely blank. My rickety office chair feels like it can barely support my weight today. I sit awkwardly for a few moments, then slowly turn on my monitor. My head stings like it is being pierced by a long, sharp needle.

Emails are piled up and waiting. Those requiring an immediate reply, others requiring my approval, and messages where I'm merely CC'ed. This work would usually take ten minutes, but today I sit and stare at it for hours. I marinade in my alcohol induced, heartbreak-infused daze all afternoon, barely pretending to be productive. What else can I do? It feels like I can't breathe right. My eyes are blurry. The pace and sharpness of my inhalations start to increase.

"Hey Youngbaek, what's wrong with you?"

Jiyoung tears me out of the staring contest I was having with my monitor.

"Um…"

"Your face is super pale. Are you sure you're okay?"

I'm suffocating. I wish I had a set of gills at the nape of my neck to get some oxygen to my brain.

"Actually… no. No, I am not."

It's probably the first time I've truly admitted this in my entire life. I'm somehow embarrassed by it. Then I turn my head and throw up. None of it makes it into the wastebasket beside my desk.

"Whoa, Youngbaek! Don't move! Oh, man!"

"What's going on over there? Huh?! Is it you again Youngbaek?"

Our team leader, listening from the other side of the cubicle partition, walks over to take a look at the mess I am.

"I'm... I'm sorry? I don't think I'm feeling well."

"No, now's not the time for sorry. Are you sure you don't need to see a doctor or something?"

I can feel the tears welling up in my eyes and am suddenly mortified by the thought of everyone seeing me cry at work. I look up at my team leader.

"If it's okay with you, I'd like to get cleaned up and then talk to you about it, um... later... at your desk."

"Sure, whatever. Go get some fresh air and please, pull yourself together."

"Hey Youngbaek, need someone to go with you?"

"No thanks, Jiyoung. I'll just go to the restroom for a quick breather."

I have my head propped up against the toilet seat. When did I arrive here in this stall? Green acid from my gallbladder floats along the surface of the water. After I'm done, the office somehow looks more yellow than before as I walk back to my desk. Wherever I look, little fluorescent spots and trails float in front of me.

"Take a seat, Youngbaek."

My team leader gestures for me to sit. Jiyoung stands next to him.

"Well then, what's going on with you? Are you sure you're okay?"

"Can... can I ask for a few days off?"

It just came out. Having never once taken a sick day in my five years working here, I couldn't hold it in any longer.

"I think I can guess what's going on... still, this is so sudden of you."

"Yes, I apologize."

"Well, there's nothing that urgent on your plate right now... use the rest of the day to get everything in order and make sure the others can cover for you while you're gone."

"Yes, sir."

"But, can you tell us anything about what's going on?"

"It's a... a personal matter. I'll be back to my old self soon."

"All right. Use your time off to get yourself back up on the horse. You look like you're going to pass out right here on the floor. Go see a doctor, or do a temple stay, whatever you need to do... just don't come back here looking like this."

When work finally finishes, I step out onto the street outside my building. Busy people, lonely streetlights, this is the world outside my phone. Without earbuds, I discover a world alive with the song of real things happening, moving. I board the same bus as always populated with the same riders—tired students with cram school workbooks tucked under their arms, burnt-out adults in suits, and other elderly riders who look more exhausted than all the rest. Everyone in here rides with head bowed, tapping away at a screen like pigeons pecking at crumbs.

The bus crosses over the river. Leaves floating in the water seem like posts in a feed. No, maybe it's just my situation. I'm drifting along without doing anything. Like a hand sprinkling breadcrumbs to the birds, everyone's phone seems to say to the drifting leaves,

"Why can't you go against the river's current?" At the end of the bridge, tall gray buildings look down on the bus as we pass. Every time a pigeon pecks at a piece of bread, the clink of a coin can be heard. The people in the bus peck away at the buttons on their phones, liking, subscribing, reposting...

Beyond the darkened window, the electronic sirens in advertisements sing at me again. *Look over here. I can give you what everyone else has. All you need to do is give us what we want. If you're willing to pay, you too can be like everyone else.*

I get off the bus and walk along the street. A multitude of other ordinary office workers just like me head to their homes, taking the same path they've taken thousands of times. I pass once more through the open-air market with stalls advertising their wares stretching out on either side of the narrow road.

"Strawberries! One basket for eight dollars! Get your strawberries!"

"You heard it. Fresh strawberries. Just eight dollars each!"

"Come on folks! Pork belly! Pork belly, by the pound. Just eighteen dollars!"

"Hey, you, there! Come take a look. Don't want to go home empty-handed do you?"

A man on a motorcycle, probably some low-paid part-timer, drives by and showers the street with flyers that no one will ever read. A sudden gust of wind sweeps the scattered flyers and trash across the road. My eyebrows furrow. A sadness hangs over me. A poster gets wrapped around my ankle and sticks to the bottom of my shoe. Hey, you piece of trash, let go! What? Do you think you and I are the same? When I get home I have to peel off another printed ad taped to the front of my door. Back in the purple-hued shadow of my apartment, I feel like I'm choking, as though breathing in water. I sink into the silence of the room.

Thanks to having no battery on my phone earlier, I ended up going on a bus tour of Seoul today, along the same route I always ride on but never bothered to really look at. As soon as I connect it to a power source, I feel like there is so much we have to catch up on. My lonely thumbs have a lot to say. They are my phone's best friends, after all. With a mind of their own, they nimbly swipe their way to the SCR33N app and open it. Like opening the screen door of a house and walking outside, the online posts form a sort of cyber swap meet, with posts lining either side of the street and stretching out into infinity like the tracks of a train. No matter how long I swipe through the feed, there is a ceaseless stream of self-aggrandizing posts, endlessly colorful and phony.

Hello! I'm in my early thirties, single, and looking for that special someone.

Hi! Everyone says I'm a real catch. DM me to find out why.

Look out, ladies. I'm in my early thirties and have about half a million in assets.

I may be in my thirties, but I try to learn something new and improve myself every day.

I'm looking to get married ASAP. Are any eligible ladies out there in their early thirties looking for a husband?

How do I measure up to other people in their thirties? I'd say I'm in the top one percent!

I'm in my early thirties and confident I've got the right specs. Go ahead, rate me!

I'm in my early thirties and not sure if I've got the right qualifications. How would you rate me?

Like hawkers selling their goods, everyone always tries so hard to present themselves in the best possible light. Imagining myself walking through this online marketplace of people, I swipe deeper and deeper into the feed. I think about how I would stand up to their descriptions of themselves, hopeful that I, too, am making myself appear desirable. Staring down this interminable railway of self-advertisement I realize a few things:

Everyone wants to get into the same universities everyone else tries to get into.

Everyone tries to work at the same companies everyone else tries to work for.

Everyone has the same relationship goals everyone else has.

I need to remove all the barriers blocking me from living the life I want to live.

I need to stop comparing myself to others and trying to be like everybody else.

I need to remove all the filters that have been placed in front of me and prevent me from loving myself and those around me.

I need to delete SCR33N.

Considering these things, staring down at the screen in my hand, my phone suddenly vibrates. It beckons to me, illuminating one-half of the room as it lights up with an incoming message. I roll over eager to see who it is.

- *Notice of Change to Your Loan Interest Rate*
- *Greetings, we are writing to notify you that as of today, the interest rate on your loan with Shilla Bank has officially been modified. As always, thank you for choosing to do business with us.*
- *Previous rate: 5.76%*
- *Modified rate as of today: 8.04%*

Bang!

Hey, phones are stronger than they look. The hollow wall of my apartment didn't fare as well. I can see pink insulation sticking out of a phone-sized hole. I reach into the wall and grab my phone out by the scruff of its neck.

Bang! Bang! Bang!

The screen of my phone shatters into jagged fragments of glass and plastic with a crackling sound. This thing that divided the world into two is broken into a hundred little pieces. A dark smear of blood can be seen between the geometric glass shards. I remove a few pieces of glass stuck in my right hand.

It's... it's not my fault. None of this. I was just at the wrong beach when the tsunami hit. Looming there in the distance for so long, that when the wave finally reached the shore, I was just standing, staring up at the pretty clouds.

I go outside to clear my head. Walking through an intersection bathed in the orange light of a street lamp, I pause to sit at the bus stop. I notice a small yellow cram school bus across the street with a banner running down its side.

You'll need an elegant solution to stay competitive in the educational environment of tomorrow! We guarantee our methods will get you into Sky University. No, really–trust us!

I can see myself twenty years earlier riding that same yellow bus every evening after regular school. Another innocent student trying to get a leg up in the gamble his poor parents made on his future. Back then, I pushed the revolving door of my cram school every evening just like I do every morning at the office, praying each time the weight of those doors would swing back and propel me to a better tomorrow. Like a piece of gum smashed into the pavement by the wheel of a car, my head gets pushed lower and lower with each revolution while I wait for a single moment to catch my breath.

I go back inside and lie down. The weak fluorescent ceiling light flashes a couple of times before illuminating the room. I lose myself in time. I move around my apartment aimlessly, groping through my bookcase. My hands come to rest on an old diary among the dusty books. As I pull it from the shelf, it automatically opens to the final entry, as though it was sitting there all this time waiting to be opened.

Am I brave enough to let go of this cliff I'm hanging onto?

My eyes start to water up, full of bitter tears. In all the years I've been alive, I've always backed away from that cliff. Even when I'd given up all hope, my courage never failed me. The emerald light of early dawn washes across the tear stains on my pillow.

A Mirror for The Blind

A narrow strip of stone-paved walkway covered in pine needles stretches along a dirt path. Walking over the smooth stones, I notice a turtle-shaped fountain spurting water from its mouth. The water makes a pleasant tinkling sound as it falls into a stone basin. The foundations look so ancient, they seem about to collapse, worn thin by the constant stream. I take a sip of water from the fountain using a small wooden bowl carved from a gourd that was left there for this purpose. I scoop the cold water into my mouth. One of the people that work here looks over and starts walking in my direction.

"Hello."
"Welcome. Please follow me."

The middle-aged employee, wearing a loose-fitting and newly-made traditional Korean outfit leads me to my room behind the back of a building down a narrow path like the one before. I'm not sure if he is actually a monk or not, but his clothes and shaved head seem to suggest so. Our footsteps seem to wake the building from its quiet reverie, sitting there listening to the song of the stream. The exposed timber used in the traditional building methods for Korean architecture emits a somehow familiar smell of freshly-cut pine.

"Right, so you're all checked in and you will be staying with us for three days, right? Please take a few hours just to relax on your own. If you leave your room at around dinner time, the evening meal should be ready and waiting for you. Feel free to come and ask us if you need anything at all.'"

"Thanks."

In my room are two bottles of water, a fridge, a bed, and a simple table. Some ancient saying in Chinese characters is scribbled on what is otherwise a pristinely white wall made out of traditional mulberry paper. I throw myself across the bed. The texture and rustle of the sheets greet me reassuringly. They're somehow consoling. I stare up at the ceiling. Is this how people relax? This is how it's done, right? I mean, I came here to rest now, didn't I? What was the best way to do it? I have to stop and smile at myself for trying to optimize relaxation itself. Just take it easy.

There is nowhere to fix my gaze. It runs off of everything. The simple patterns on the ceiling are barely visible and seem to move around serenely. I feel dizzy as if drunk off the silence from being cut off from the external world. I'd like to relax. I'd like to forget about everything without a thought in my head. I don't want to remember the last time I used my phone and ended up smashing it against a wall. I also want to forget about the new phone I ordered almost immediately, even as I swept up the broken pieces of my last one. It must be in the mail and on its way to my home right now... A spectrum of different thoughts invades my mind like ink spreading in water.

I'm taken back to when I was an elementary school student, a sheet of A4 paper flapping and bending out of shape as I carried it over to my mother.

"Mom, what do you think I should be when I grow up?"

"Why? Did your teacher ask you to write down what you want to be for homework?"

"Uh-huh."

"Well, I just want you to find something that doesn't require you to toil all day long, like your father and I had to."

"What does 'toil' mean?"

"It means the sort of thing that any son of mine shouldn't have to do."

"Then, who 'toils,' mom?"

"Children who don't study hard or listen to their mothers, that's who."

A few years later, during a homeroom assembly, I remember our teacher smiling and stating that twenty out of thirty students said they wanted to be civil servants. She reminded us all that to do that you would have to forget about all the other subjects and focus as hard as you could on taking the entrance exam.

"All right everyone, just remember how important this exam will be for your future. I know I'm just an elementary homeroom teacher, but if you ever find yourself struggling in any other subjects, remember to forget all about them and just focus on the five key subjects for the test. That's all that will be on the college entrance exam, you know. Trust me, you want to work hard now so that you won't suffer later. It's never too soon to start."

Like a person afraid of going hungry and stockpiling food, throughout middle and high school we were taught to accumulate as much test knowledge through rote memorization as we could.

It wouldn't have been nearly as fun without my best friends–and toughest competition–Dongjoo and Inyoung there beside me. The three of us had been locked in a three-way tug-of-war ever since we were children. We were only kids back then, but now that we were adults there really was no excuse for constantly vying against each other the way we did. Only a few years after that, we became university students like three gangly roses growing side by side up a trellis. Then Jungyoon came into the picture like a bright pink orchid. As I sit here thinking about my past, the memories that we had together weave in and out of my mind like a red thread.

Sky University's Philosophy Department. I remember standing and staring at the horizon as if the blue sky itself would open up before me. That's where I first set out on the long, arduous path that would take me far from those rose and orchid-scented days. Saddled with new goals and expectations, I set out down a path toward employment with my dreams rattling behind me like an old keychain.

A business card with the words "Assistant Manager Youngbaek

Kim" floats down the winding river of life, sucked up into its current. With "P Corporation" written in bold letters across the front, the craft is somehow able to avoid the ever-present rocks and rapids. Then, down past the mountains of stock options and over the real estate rainbow, I finally reach the sea. But, at what cost did I receive the scars I now have?

The sun, in its endless passage overhead, will surely see me through another night and on to a new dawn. Wait... have I ever really lay still like this in a space with no connection to the outside world? I'm not dead, am I? No, I don't think so. What time is it, anyway? How long have I been laying here? All I can hear is the sound of water flowing quietly outside. There's not a hint of other people, popularity, or judgment going through my mind.

My eyes shoot wide open. I didn't know it rained this early in winter. A shower must have passed by in the night. Waking up to a new day after a night of the deepest sleep I've had in a while feels like a sponge has scrubbed my sight clean. I also feel slightly heavier as though waterlogged from being back in my body. My once-curved spine feels straight, even a bit stiff. Have I been walking around with it always feeling this way? Outside my window, the sun creeps along the lawn. All the objects in the room where I'm staying now have short, well-defined shadows attached to them. The Chinese characters on the wall, which I am still unable to decipher, have a long shadow streaking across them. I stretch and look at the world around me.

Groping my hand along the unfamiliar wall, I find the light

switch to the bathroom and turn it on. I take some of the clothes I brought with me from home and hang them on the towel rack, removing my old clothes and hanging them on the door handle. I turn on the sink and face myself in the mirror. I'm greeted by a face puffy with sleep and my lackluster upper body. I feel truly alone for the first time in as long as I can remember. Without my phone, I can't even check what people are doing or post about my temple stay on social media. I wash the sleep from my face and body with warm water, then change into comfortable clothes.

The window glows from the sunshine beating down on it. I start to feel weak with hunger. Outside, a constant jet streams from the turtle's mouth, fed through the stone conduit of its ancient and infinite water supply. Hollowed-out drinking gourds still bob on the surface of the fountain. Just where I left them. I pour some water into an ocher-colored basin, capturing the reflection of the sky. Looking down, in comparison to the vivid world around me I am taken aback by my pale face. I splash it with cool water. Off in the distance, the person who works here, now carrying a rag, calls to me in a clear voice.

"Did you sleep well? You didn't eat dinner last night. Catching up on some much-needed rest, huh?"

I cough to clear my throat, breaking my silence since yesterday. "Oh, yes. I guess it did me well."

"Well, it's almost time for breakfast. You should eat something, don't you think?"

His suggestion that I eat something feels like a gentle challenge, like testing whether I want to live or not. Hearing the word breakfast reminds me of how hungry I really am.

"By the way, I wanted to ask..."

"Yes?"

"What do those characters on the wall of my room mean?"

"Define your own self, wherever you go."

Huh? What does that mean? How can I even think about approaching how to define myself when I know I'll be going back to work in a few days?

"What is it supposed to mean?"

"That you should always strive to be the sole proprietor of your mind."

He answers this second question without even skipping a beat. I bet everyone that stays in that room asks him about this stuff.

"Oh, right. Cool saying."

After satisfying my hunger, the little thinker within me lifts his head again as though poised to say something. Are we going to see the first snow of the year pretty soon? Maybe it would be worth it to get up and go over to that big hill behind the temple while the weather's still nice... Of course, I alone am the sole proprietor of my mind. But, what did he mean by defining myself wherever I go?

I decide to hike up the nearby hill taking the dirt path. No one is waiting for me anywhere. And I wait for no one. I go at my own pace. But, what am I doing up here? Why did I decide to climb this hill in the first place? It wasn't to post about the distance I climbed. It's not like walking all this way is going to benefit me or be profitable in any way. What made me do it? Who's going to see how far I walked when I'm done? It hurts my mind to watch myself try so hard, and even find that I am enjoying myself while doing it, without expecting anything in return.

With sweat pouring down my forehead, I reach the summit of the hill. Like the bumpy, uneven underside of a crab shell, a small village stands out amidst the trees in the distance. A few twisted pines stand staring silently at each other, barely attached to the rocky surface. The pine trees almost seem like the owners of this hill. But, if one of those boulders the trees are on were to come loose...

I descend from the top by a winding path that extends out in front of me in a long, unending vein through the landscape. What really made me decide to climb up here? I imagine myself replying to these questions as though I were answering an interview with a reporter. "Well, simply because the sky called to me, I guess." I smile and chuckle a bit with no one to see but me, envisioning myself as the main character in an Albert Camus novel.

When I get down, I ask myself again. Youngbaek, why did you climb that hill today?

The entrance to my accommodation in the distance is a welcome sight to my tired legs. I take a deep breath in front of my room. Then I open the door and walk through. The rustic walls seem to encase me. The Chinese characters look at me with a friendly grin, seeming to say: "So, you finally learned my name, huh?" No, not yet. I have no idea what you mean. Out of the corner of my eye, I spot the sun clinging to the top of the hill in the distance. Seeing those crooked pine trees at the summit takes away some of the tiredness in my legs.

The sun rises high in the sky as it nears the middle of the day. I leave the front door of my room open to the breeze and sit down on the patio. Except for the few scattered pines, the hill stands nearly bare in the early winter. Only the evergreens stand at the peak like generals. I spot an oak tree with a bit of foliage left on it and an alder wrapped in vines standing at an impossible angle. I bow down to put my shoes back on. I took them off in such a hurry that the right shoe is where the left one should be. They stare innocently back up at me.

On the day I go back to work, I catch a faint smell of the dirty rag I used to clean the floor of my apartment. Then, I walk out of the door with my newly-ordered phone in hand. I look again at the worn-out numbers of the keypad on my door lock.

Dark clouds this early in the morning seem to forecast rain later today. None of the other passengers on the bus say a word to one another. I scan through the news on social media, searching for familiar faces. Dongjoo made a big post about how he's quitting social media altogether. We'll see how long that lasts... There's a post by Inyoung that comes right after Dongjoo's that I can't help but laugh out loud at. She's wondering if anyone has ever used a matchmaking service before. Apparently, she needs pointers on setting up a profile.

Just like every other day, everyone is back at it, pushing their heavy stones up their never-ending hills. I reach the revolving doors of my company and push my particular stone as hard as I can.

"Look who's back safe and sound. Good morning!"

Jiyoung greets me with her usual energy.

"Is that Youngbaek? You're back I see."

My team leader seems less happy to see me, but also chimes in with a degree of concern.

"We thought you were going to die the other day. Glad to see you're looking better. Much better, in fact."

"Just so you know, Jungwoo got into an accident over the weekend. If you get the chance, you should go see him at the hospital."

"What?!"

"Apparently, one of his hobbies was motorcycles or something. Beats me how a guy like Jungwoo could have a hobby like that. Anyway, we made a visiting schedule at the office to show our support. Anyone can take time off to go."

I clear away some piles of papers that accumulated on my desk while I was away. After dusting off the area, I toss the wet wipes I use in the trash, then turn on my computer. Slowly one, then two, then dozens of emails queue up in my inbox, waiting for replies. Why am I unsurprised that right at its onset, my day is already starting to slip away from me?

At 6 p.m., I arrive in front of the hospital where Jungwoo is after leaving work. Patients in medical scrubs shuffle around in front of the hospital with IV poles in tow. I pass by the emergency room, then the hospital mortuary, and go through a set of revolving doors to the general care unit. I see people waiting in wheelchairs or sitting around coffee tables for their

numbers to be called. I look up where they said Jungwoo would be and make my way over to his room. In front of the elevator, a hospital employee loudly clicks a ballpoint pen, asks for my name, and then writes it down in the visitation log.

Overhead fluorescent strips light up the ward like beacons. I ask a nurse who looks like he's limping under the stress of the day where Jungwoo is. Without stopping, he points me down the hall, then disappears around the corner. There are four names next to the door. One of them is Jungwoo Lee. I push the door open and step into the room.

A middle-aged woman in her fifties wearing wrinkled clothes sits next to the bed with Jungwoo's chart and name tag. She looks strangely familiar, like I've seen her somewhere.

"Hello, are you here to visit?"

"Yes, um... hi. My name is Youngbaek Kim. I work with Jungwoo at P Corporation."

"So, you're Youngbaek. I'm Jungwoo's mother. He mentioned that you might be stopping by. They took him to get some tests done, I think."

"Oh, I see."

While I look for a place to put the fruit basket I brought, Jungwoo's mom gets up from her folding chair and starts to talk to me. She bows way lower than is required in this sort of situation, and I wonder if she recognizes me from somewhere. I notice that she has callouses all over her hands. They were definitely not Gangnam hands.

"I'm so glad Jungwoo has someone like you at the office to watch over him."

"Of course, but how did Jungwoo... ?"

"Oh, well you know how hardworking my son is. I mean, he would stay up all night studying and working until the morning. Then, the other night he was making a delivery on his Vespa, and well... he had an accident."

I imagine Jungwoo's bland expression, his plain, guileless way of talking, then remember a blue bike helmet I could have sworn I saw him wear somewhere... Jungwoo's mother seems like she's struggling to find the words to say something else that's on the tip of her tongue.

"Maybe you don't recognize me like this, but I've seen you around the office from time to time. I do some cleaning work for P Corporation."

A bed is rolled into the room with a rattling sound. Jungwoo, with both of his arms wrapped tightly to his sides, is lying in the middle. An array of different hoses for sustenance or for urine are connected in a tangled mess across his body. Jungwoo manages to open his eyes on his bruised and swollen face, which forms into a slight, crescent smile. I guess he hasn't been able to shave in here, so the few black dots of his beard and mustache punctuate the expression.

"Youngbaek!"

A bit of sunlight pools in the shadows under Jungwoo's eyes.

"Hey. How... how are you, Jungwoo? You seem better than I thought you would."

"Grateful that you came. Can I offer you something to drink?"

For a moment, I'm in awe that even in a hospital bed Jungwoo can be so polite. Gesturing at the fruit basket, Jungwoo's mom stands up and excuses herself.

"I just have something to see to something outside... You two go ahead and talk."

Jungwoo bows his head a fraction, thanking her like any good son would, and motions with his eyes towards the door. When his mother leaves, I go over and sit in the folding chair.

"You broke your arm too, huh? I'm so sorry this happened, Jungwoo."

"Well, my mom is helping out as best she can."

"I'm just glad you seem to be in such good spirits."

"Ha! At least I have a good excuse not to have to go to work."

All right then, since he seems okay, maybe it's a good time to prod him a little about this delivery and real estate stuff...

"How long have you been riding, um... motorcycles, anyway?"

"It started in college. This isn't even the first time I crashed. I've been hurt a few times. Ha, ha... you know how it goes..."

Another simple and straightforward answer from Jungwoo, only this time I know that it's a bald-faced lie. Sad that I had to hear it from his own mother that he was out making chicken deliveries on his Vespa instead of zipping around like some hotshot Gangnam biker.

I can hear the news playing on TV out in the waiting room. For a moment, I listen to it intently. There's something in the urgency of the news caster's tone that suggests they are about to announce some breaking news, which draws my attention from Jungwoo's bed.

"In other news... The famous online personality and finance guru, known as *"Val-You"* has been charged with market manipulation with regard to his fraudulent management of online communities related to the stock exchange. In addition to his popular video channel, *"Val-You"* was apparently known for actively recommending specific stocks to the general public through private messaging apps. An intensive investigation is currently underway centered around his involvement in a private subscription and consulting scam that goes by the name, *'Val-You Together'.*"

Jungwoo blinks, then closes his eyes as though there is something to be grateful for in the news coming from down the hall.

"... all right then, Jungwoo. I'm glad I came to see you. It's getting late, so I better let you relax. I'll be in touch. Hang in there, man."

"Thanks, Youngbaek. I really appreciate you coming."

I leave the hospital. At first I feel light-hearted, relieved by the fact that someone who seemed as well-adjusted as Jungwoo was actually exactly like me behind it all. Then I feel a certain heaviness in my chest. All those thoughts that I was able to escape during my retreat start flooding back in. Neon lights and electronic signs outside of shops line the side of the road, their loud advertisements flashing before my eyes.

I wait at the crosswalk. People with earbuds stare down at the screens in their palms. "How are you really doing today, Young-baek?" my new phone seems to ask me as it vibrates its hard, plastic body convulsing in my pocket. Take me out and look at me. You know you want to! Inside its perfectly rectangular mirror, I see the reflection of my expressionless face. As I slide my phone back into my pocket and start walking across the street, I notice that I've missed my signal in the time it took to look down at my phone.

A car crosses the intersection just as I am about to step down from the curb. That was close. Then, another person suddenly comes up from behind and walks straight out into the street. Head down and listening to music, he walks obliviously into the oncoming traffic.

"Just a moment!"

A speeding van nearly hits him. Its horn blares off into the distance. He steps back to the curb with a low gasp. A few beads of sweat dot his forehead and he flashes an embarrassed smile. The light turns green.

I get on the bus headed home. Each person looks down at their own mirror, sitting side by side in their chairs like sparrows perched on a wire. The sound of an advertisement jingle announces the bus's departure.

"Do you want to work far away or close to Seoul? Become a first-rate marriageable candidate on your way to becoming a civil servant. There is no employment quite as elegant as this!"

I close my eyes and see someone tall, someone with an apartment in Gangnam, someone who never loses their composure, someone who is always agreeable, no matter what... The people in my life appear before me. I shake my head, then squeeze my eyes tighter. I see a white and haggard face over a sink staring back at me in the mirror. It's cold when I get back to my apartment. The hands of my clock trace the same trajectory over a disk of ceaseless time. It hangs over an arch in the entranceway and I nearly hit my head on the bottom of it for the thousandth time. I should really move that thing. I feel thirty-two years old.

"You, too, have the *'val-You'* to make it big! Hello everyone and a big welcome to all my subscribers out there! I'm streaming this video live as a special episode to share what I've been up to!"

His familiar voice comes from my phone. Funny, I don't even

remember opening the video app. When I pick it up to look, I see a bank account number written in a big yellow box in the top-right corner of the screen.

"I'm putting my personal account number up on the screen. I'm sure you've all heard the news, and while I'm legally barred from saying anything about the investigation at this point in time, trust me when I say that with your help and financial contributions, we will be able to overcome this together. Donate now to invest in the future of this channel, your own financial future, and the future of our great nation. Thank you."

As always, Mr. Jung–I mean *Val-You* seems to be firing away words like a machine gun with his hearty voice and contagious laughter.

"With that aside, I'm super excited to announce today's special guest! She is none other than the star instructor from *the Elegant Education and Employment Consulting firm*, Ms. Sora Kim! Please give her a warm welcome!"

"Hi, hello! Thanks for having me. Let me start by saying that success is all just a state of mind And *that* is what elegance is all about!"

Fine wrinkles now lined her face since she taught us mathematics at her cram school. Since then, the motto, 'Success is a state of mind' had emerged as the new catchphrase of the *'Elegant* Academy.'

"Let me tell you, with things the way they are, it's just such a godsend that you're here. Now, I know you're great at teaching, but tell me, are you good at real estate too?"

"I actually have a lot to say about this. All of you young people out there... you think you can't afford a house, right? Well, I'm here to tell you that if you just study a little bit about real estate every day you, too, can get there. The problem is, you don't study! That's right. You all are too busy going out on dates instead of investing in your financial future! It isn't about how much you have in the bank—not at all! It's all about how you perceive yourself in your mind. Having this sort of weak mentality is another typical trait of the poor."

"Wow, did you hear that? And I thought she was only good at giving lectures. It sounds like she's also a savvy investor! Hey there, that's my specialty. Ha! Ha! But tell me, if everyone stops going out on dates, won't the fertility rate fall even more? I mean, who is going to invest if there are no more young people?"

The star instructor of Elegant Academy tries to mask her annoyance at this sudden challenge to what she just said with a bright smile on her face.

"Oh, is that how you see it? As always, Val-You seems to be going on about something only he understands. No wonder your channel has over a million subscribers."

I'm not sure if her envy is genuine or if she's trying to mock him. Blowing past her ambiguous words, Val-You continues with his usual confidence.

"Look, all I'm saying is that two successful, financially free people like us should be the ones openly discussing such significant societal issues. Don't you think?"

Her voice brims with confidence, as though reciting a proclamation. She seems relieved to be back on *Val-You*'s team.

"*Val-You*! Be careful with those statements; our viewers might hit the unsubscribe button, you know? Haha."

"No, not at all, my friend. I believe the people who subscribe to this channel understand both their 'value' and our 'value' very clearly."

"You always have such powerful and motivating words to say."

"How about we take a short break here and continue afterward? Next, we'll discuss the relationship between birth rates and real estate prices!"

"See you in a while!"

I open the window. Outside, I hear the faint sound of music and people talking underneath the light of a neon sign. I toss my phone on the bed.

Then I take out my old diary from the bookshelf. I skim through the entries. There are doodles scrawled over some pages. I examine some of the worn photos stuck between the pages. I turn one more time to the last page. The one about hanging from the cliff. Then, when I turn to the next clean page it is as though I do fall off the cliff into a white abyss.

I grab a ballpoint pen from my desk. Then draw a rectangle mirror, using a single, wobbling line. I fill in the empty space to the point where the paper is ready to rip, heavy with ink. Then

I fill in the screen by drawing neat barcode-like lines, layer after layer. Youngbaek Kim, Dongjoo Lee, Inyoung Choi, Jungwoo Lee, Jiyoung Kim... I write each name on top of the other until they are indistinguishable from one another, just a single black blot.

The sun will keep rising and I'll still be standing with my head bowed over, squinting at the sunlight reflected on the screen of my phone. It's getting late now and the night has a while left to go before the sun stretches across the horizon and announces a new tomorrow.

The end.

About the Author

The author, Jeong Mu, majored in physics and then worked as a software engineer at a large Korean company. Since 2023, he started working as commissioner at the Seoul Youth Policy Network. His first novel, A Mirror for the Blind, has been widely acclaimed in Korean literary circles for its raw portrayal of Korea's harsh working culture, declining fertility rate, and high suicide rates, providing an insider's look into what makes Korea tick.

www.ingramcontent.com/pod-product-compliance
Lightning Source LLC
LaVergne TN
LVHW041803060526
838201LV00046B/1112